D1738543

TABLE OF CONTENTS

ACKNOWLEDGEMENTS

I believe that nothing in this world is created without the help of the collective human consciousness and support of like-minded individuals. This book is a personal representation of my appreciation toward each one of my teachers, mentors, friends, and readers.

I AM so very grateful for God's inspiration, His creative force & energy which gave me the idea and inspired me to write this work. It has allowed me to become aware of who I truly am— a channel of communication to help deliver the powerful and transformative information found in this book.

I feel blessed for the opportunity to learn from some of the most influential and brilliant minds from around the world and the privilege to learn from extraordinary spiritual masters, religious leaders, inventors, and philosophers — and from science itself. I will always be grateful to my teachers who have contributed to helping me find my path; some who I have met, some who I have not. Many of my teachers have become treasured personal friends.

I give special thanks to those who have attended my seminars and afforded me the privilege of discovering of my life's purpose and meaning through them.

The universe has provided a challenging, yet purposeful journey which has influenced both how I view the world as well as how I choose to live in it. Through this journey I have discovered my life's purpose to help others become aware and realize their unlimited Divine power and infinite potential to achieve true prosperity—in the form of authentic happiness, joy, and financial freedom (or whatever their heart desires).

I am such a lucky and blessed man to have a wonderful family from the start. My brothers, sister, and their families have always supported me whether I was up or down in my life. That deep gratitude extends to my father and mother for their love, support and beautiful spirits. I will forever be grateful to Kathy Esfahani, for being a wonderful mother to our two beautiful daughters, Kristina and Alisha. I am so very grateful for the deep love & joy in having our granddaughter, Haven Rose. Furthermore, I am proud and grateful for each of my daughter's husbands, Logan and Joey.

Words cannot describe how lucky and blessed I am to have the most supportive, understanding, loving and beautiful wife, Ann. I am also so very grateful for the love and support from our family, Amr, Karim and Nadine.

I offer a special note of appreciation to my editor, Belinda Casper, for your kindness, support, competence and contribution to my work. Your guidance has been outstanding, and I am so grateful and thankful for you. I want to provide an additional note of thanks for Curt Coenen's proofreading and support.

I believe there are no accidents in life. You are reading this book because it is meant for you at this time in your life. You are ready for this powerful information and knowledge to transform and impact your life. I welcome you to my world and to your new exciting world.

The journey begins! Let's transform the world together by first transforming ourselves. Together we can make the world we live in a better place, which therefore will make the world a better place for everyone.

INTRODUCTION

Have you ever wondered how it would feel to have true freedom? What it would be like to live the life you want? Drive the car of your choice? Travel and explore the world? Easily provide your kids and family with the best life has to offer? All while being able to live, work, and play from anywhere you choose?

I truly believe we can all live the life of our dreams. And, YES, you can too! Before we start this journey, you should ask yourself these questions:

1. What if it is true that we have Divine power within us to use to connect with for our benefit?
2. What if it is true that our paradigm (belief system) controls all aspects of our life? Then, how would our paradigm affect us and our families?
3. What if it is true that we can change our paradigm to control and transform our lives?

That leads us to ask even better questions... What would be the cost if we don't take advantage of this powerful system to transform our lives? What responsibilities do we have to ourselves, families, friends, and the whole world to share this powerful information for transformation and prosperity?

Along my own personal journey to prosperity, I attended several different personal development seminars and workshops and read hundreds of self-help books. What I discovered is many presenters and authors would tell you "WHAT" you needed to succeed, but they didn't teach you

"HOW" to do it. They would say "You must have the right mindset in order to accomplish what you want in life."

That's great, but what is the 'right mindset?' *How* do I change and shift my mindset? *How* do I do 'the right' thing in the 'right' order at the 'right' time to shift my consciousness? After these workshops I was left with a feeling of excitement and motivation, only to realize I didn't quite have the tangible tools to actualize and achieve my goals. As such, I would get discouraged and eventually lose focus and momentum.

While many of these personalities were very experienced and respected within their niche, many of them presented concepts that came only from books—rather than from their own personal experiences. This book is a product of *real-life* experiences. I have been at the top of the mountain, just as I have been at the lowest point of the valley. I am not a professor of any kind, nor am I a psychologist. My qualifications are even more profound...I am nothing more than an ordinary dreamer who was willing to believe I could be extraordinary. It was my willingness to be extraordinary, my vision of prosperity and a high level of awareness that allowed me to become an expert on teaching mind-power techniques.

The idea of prosperity is much more than just a concept of money. It's about how you define abundance in your life. This book is about learning how to bring true abundance and prosperity into your life!

This book will reveal a step-by-step system to give you the tools to activate and open your mind and heart to prosperity through the power of the mind. What it all boils down to is the idea you are only as prosperous as the level of prosperity you are currently experiencing. This comprises all aspects of your life from your health, happiness, and relationships, to your sense of personal peace and abundance. Moreover, you can only experience a higher level of prosperity if you are open to it and intend on living it. You can't be completely abundant if you continue to tell yourself limiting statements or maintain limiting beliefs.

This system is about lasting transformation. You will receive specific instructions on how to control and design a prosperity mindset in your life—and most importantly—how to actively implement the system to achieve maximum transformation.

It's about the story between your two ears (your mindset). These stories determine who you become in life.

My mission is to help people from all walks of life experience a higher level of awareness and discover their own Divine, hidden power already within them. I want to teach them exactly how to use the Divine power to create *ANYTHING* they want in life. Discovering this Divine power will make a *HUGE DIFFERNCE* in their lives.

So, how is this done? I teach and train entrepreneurs as well as future entrepreneurs to boost their awareness and confidence by sharing specific proven tools and strategies which help them achieve more powerful and measurable *RESULTS* in their own authentic way, in order to ultimately boost their income — which makes a profound impact on their lives and the way they live them.

This knowledge and powerful system is for you, if you:
- ✓ Feel stuck.
- ✓ Don't know where to start, but know you need to make a change in your life.
- ✓ You're constantly starting over and getting nowhere.
- ✓ Don't have time to read a ton of books to find the answers.
- ✓ Don't already have the strategies or techniques to control your paradigm (mindset, beliefs).
- ✓ Feel anxious time is passing too so fast and you are worried about your future.

✓   You have no clear plans or direction to be financially independent.

Should you choose to follow the systems and techniques in this book, I am confident you will find clarity, purpose, and direction in any and all areas of your life. If your purpose in reading this book is to earn more money, then you will discover the tools and techniques on how to boost your mind power and creative thinking abilities that will translate into earning more money.

If you are an executive, entrepreneur, in sales, or a leader in the direct selling industry with an organization of your own, you will boost your business to a whole new level of success by infusing these ideas into your strategy. You will also know how to lead your teams to do the same, regardless of your industry!

This system can also be used to obtain more health and happiness, as well as to foster meaningful relationships. Moreover, you will notice after reading and implementing this system, you will become a person of high awareness and influence. You will be more efficient, disciplined, focused, productive, and find yourself developing better time management and decision-making skills. Above all, it will help you gain more confidence and a higher level of awareness. All of this can be yours when you follow and apply the system.

This is not your typical book. It is a step-by-step manuscript containing specific keys to help you open the door to prosperity. It is a book about the "*HOW*."

In the following chapters, I will teach you how to prepare your mind and heart to be open to prosperity. As you go through this system, I will bring your attention to many key points and truths. When you understand them, you will possess the master key to your life of prosperity (or whatever it is you desire).

My passion and purpose of this book is to transfer this powerful knowledge to the maximum number of people from all walks of life, age, gender, and culture to transform their lives, and that of the human consciousness, in a positive way.

I invite you to read this book and put the system into practice to see yourself prosper and live the life you were meant to live!

CHAPTER ONE
Your Secret, Hidden Divine Power

You may or may not be aware you have Divine power within you—a secret, hidden power. I am about to share with you powerful information that may shock you but will certainly benefit you in very positive ways.

Your Divine hidden power provides knowledge, insights, ideas, principles, tools, wisdom, and techniques which are far more than just interesting information or motivation. It contains pivotal and powerful knowledge that will unlock the power of your true potential and has the capability to impact and change many lives, including yours.

I wrote this book with a focus on prosperity and entrepreneurship because I am very passionate about building big businesses and helping others to do the same. However, you can use these same tools to attract anything you want in life too! The tools could be used to improve your health, find a partner, and more. It's up to you to determine what it is you want and apply the tools and system to get it!

Personally, I love the process of manifesting and creating. I am an entrepreneur myself and have seen the power of tapping into my "Divine Power" to achieve great success. I know just about everyone wants (or wishes) to be an *entrepreneur* because humans are wired to always grow and expand; to live the best life has to offer. But not everyone knows the steps to take to reach this success. This book will teach you these steps.

In order to truly be or become an *entrepreneur*, it is essential to have the *right mindset*; aligned with what you want to achieve.

Together, the mind and body create the perfect natural balance which alters our internal health and state-of-mind to a whole new state of *being*. Furthermore, they rely on one another: *The body requires energy from the mind to physically carry out its mission and responsibilities to accomplish the goals and desires we have in life.*

CHAPTER TWO
Discovering the Prosperity System

I was 19 years of age when I first came to the United States. It was 1976 when I traveled to Detroit, Michigan as a teenager with very little money, little knowledge of the English language, and no clear direction regarding what to do next. The only thing I brought with me was a dream about the "land of opportunity," and more importantly, my hunger to discover the secret to happiness, health, success, and prosperity.

I believed by faithfully seeking those desires, I would find success. It became second nature for me to explore every piece of information about life and business by reading books, attending self-development seminars, and listening and learning from coaches and mentors who had real-life experiences. During these difficult times, it was my open mind and willingness to learn from others that kept me going. Before I knew it, I had a grasp of the English language and was working several jobs. I then began to pursue a degree in electrical engineering at Wayne State University.

One day, I was sitting in class and had a strange, overwhelming feeling. This strange feeling quickly changed to clarity as I realized it was my intuition, rather than just a random feeling. The message echoing in my mind was so clear. I knew what I was to do next, and it would change my life forever. My intuition urged me to make a change. It was telling me *"this isn't you. You're not destined for a life as an electrical engineer. Something greater awaits."*

At the time, it seemed crazy, especially since I was only three months away from graduation, but somehow deep inside I knew this wasn't my path. So, at that very moment, I listened to that feeling—that intuition—and got up from my chair, left the classroom, and never returned.

Everyone around me, including my parents, thought I was crazy, and tried to convince me to change my mind, but I had made my choice and I somehow just *knew* it was right.

That's not to say it was easy. After I walked out the door of that classroom, I didn't exactly know what to do next. The only thing I *did* know was I wanted to be my own boss, though admittedly, I didn't know how to accomplish it—yet. For the time being I was a college dropout who was confused and had very little money to my name. To keep myself afloat, I continued my job on an assembly line for Chrysler, which I hated, but it paid the bills.

When the Student is Ready, the Teacher Will Appear
In 1981 I moved to Atlanta, Georgia and found work as a front office clerk at the Atlanta Hilton and Towers Hotel. Within three months I was promoted to the disco bar manager, and then after six months, something happened which only God could have orchestrated. I met a nice gentleman who would have a profound impact on me and the direction of my life. This man, a very successful real estate broker in Atlanta, seemed to take an interest in me and before long, our casual acquaintance grew into a business relationship where I found myself being coached, mentored and groomed for success in the real estate industry by this inspiring individual. I was able to create my first little empire in the real estate business. I will forever be grateful for the opportunity to learn from such a knowledgeable man, not only because he helped me take my first steps towards taking control over my life, but also because he challenged me to look inwards for the answers. I can still hear his voice echoing in my mind, "*If you want to understand others and how the Universe works, you must first understand*

14

yourself." Since then, I never stopped learning or investing in myself to continuously work to boost the level of my awareness and personal mind power.

You Must Have a Clear Vision of Where You're Going

Fast forward many years later to the summer of 1992, I found myself taking a moment as I always do to be thankful for what I achieved in the last sixteen years since coming to the United States. I had just about everything I wanted; family, a big house, luxurious cars, flashy country club memberships, a lot of money, friends, personal power, and a great lifestyle. In short, I was living a prosperous life.

Then it hit me. It was like flash of light that woke me from a deep sleep. There it was again—that strong, overwhelming feeling I had back in college. It was my intuition—except this time, it wasn't a feeling; it was a vision. In one exhilarating moment, sixteen years passed before my eyes as my conscious mind whizzed with questions, *How had I accomplished this success in my life? How blessed was I? How had my life been transformed in such a big way?* Meanwhile, my intuition continued to flash vivid images across my thoughts and then, almost as fast as it had started, it stopped. I sat there speechless. I had my answers. I had *become* the person I had wanted to be so many years ago, just by *visualizing and feeling it.* I had somehow tapped into my subconscious mind and manifested my dreams into reality. I realized everything I had accomplished in my life had once began as a goal and the person I wanted to become was simply an image I had already painted in my mind.

As I sat there contemplating what just happened, it occurred to me, when I was younger, I was simply pre-playing the future (thinking, visualizing and feeling) the things I wanted to achieve in life and business in my mind's eye. That day, I learned how to manifest anything I wanted in life into existence, simply through my secret power hidden deep inside me. My intuition gently reaffirmed the need to have a clear

15

vision of where you're going in order to get where you want to go.

When It Rains, It Pours

As you learn more about my journey, you will come to understand the ways in which the universe has been preparing me for my role in its Divine plan. You see, while I have been truly blessed with a life of prosperity, along my journey there have been many ups and downs, and serious challenges along the way too.

One example along my journey in life was the collapse of the real estate and financial markets during the recession which started in 2008. Up until that point, I was living a comfortable, even wealthy lifestyle. When the market crashed, I went bankrupt and lost everything. Not only had I lost everything financially, but I also lost something even more precious; the life of a very dear friend and business partner to cancer. As they say, "when it rains, it pours," and I was stuck in the middle of a financial and personal storm.

I knew I wasn't the only one in trouble. The banks were tanking too, which caused an uproar of chaos within the economy. In my mind the *banks* were to blame for the root of all of my troubles. At least that's what I told myself at the time. I had to blame someone! None of what was happening seemed real, and while on the outside I tried to be "Mr. Positive," the reality was I simply wasn't ready to face the truth: Everything I had worked for was gone.

This fact attacked my pride and sent my psyche down a vicious path of self-destruction and fear. Meanwhile, I was forced to swallow my pride and ask my friends and family for money— just to get by. This only added to my embarrassment. I was stuck in a vicious circle of blaming myself and the economy for my misfortune. I just couldn't find a way out of the hole I had found myself in.

It took almost three years for the bank to finally foreclose on my house and other assets. The good news, though I couldn't see it at the time, was the courts were exceedingly busy handling the highest influx of bankruptcy filings ever recorded in US history. Because it was a long, drawn-out process, it forced me into what I referred to as my "isolation period of self-discovery." The silver lining in all of this was I had time to realize what I had done by allowing myself to get caught up in the mindset of the time.

I learned the same tools applied to create the life you wanted, can also impact you negatively when your mindset is one of fear!

It was during this time my wife and I decided to pack up what little we had left and move to St. Petersburg, Florida, where we found a meager, yet comfortable 400-square-foot apartment. Once we settled in, I finally had time to process everything that had happened. I began to recall the advice my mentor had given me about seeking the answers within. If I wanted to understand why this had happened, not only to me, but to the entire economy, I had to first understand myself.

Through much introspection, I finally realized what had happened. In the years leading up to the economic collapse of 2008, we as a collective society felt the negative energy surrounding the economy. The media kept broadcasting about how bad things were. . . consumer confidence was at an all-time low, the bank system was tanking, and the future of the economy looked bleak. Even within the real estate industry, developers were canceling pending contracts and were certainly not interested in pursuing new ones. Everywhere I went, whether it was to a private club, restaurant, coffee shop, or just the grocery store, there was inescapable chatter about how bad things were and how much worse they were going to become.

Inevitably, despite all I knew about the power of the mind and how I had used it to become successful in the first place, I fed into the negativity with the fear of losing my financial empire. As soon as I fell victim to it, I lost access to my secret, hidden power, and replaced it with fear in my conscious mind. I embodied this collective fear, worry, and doubt. Before long, those thoughts became my reality. I had manifested my own downfall and destruction!

Imagine it! I had used so much positive energy and thinking to build the life I wanted, and then I completely went away from it and lost it all. *Why hadn't I stopped it and changed my course?*

It's good to remember, at times fear will show up in our lives. But when we begin playing a mental slideshow of how things *might look and feel*, if all the news and chatter were true, we will attract the same negative things you're fearing.

In the end, I realized the crisis of 2008 was nothing more than a mass psychological effect, and I too fell for it, even though I knew better.

Something Lost, Something Gained

Deep down inside my heart, even amidst all my challenges and losses, I knew everything was going to be fine, and everything happened for a good reason. How did I know that? It came from my ability to be open and aware of our oneness with God, and how we manifest our realities through our thoughts and beliefs.

My experience through the rise and demise of my financial empire during the recession of 2008 proved this power within us works *both* ways—in building the good and the not so good. What you think and believe *will* come to pass and you have unlimited potential to transform your life.

The realization life is nothing more than a manifestation of our thoughts and beliefs took on a whole new meaning the second time around. When I first experienced it, I only knew what it meant to manifest the *good* (health, wealth, and happiness).

The second time, however, I understood what it felt like to manifest *the not so good (*fear, pain and grief*).*

I gained so much power and awareness from what I thought was a loss. Through this experience, I reached new levels of awakening and awareness and deepened my understanding of the secret, hidden power within me...The power to create and control my reality.

The Missing Piece

We hear so much about the idea we all have "a Divine power within us." Have you ever wondered if you *truly* have a power within you? What does it mean? How can you access it? How can it impact your life? You are about to discover how prosperous and top achievers think and act by accessing and utilizing their inner power. This system will help you become familiar with how your mind processes information in order to get what you want. It is not only about what to do and what needs to be done, it is about *HOW* to do it!

Our belief system is like the software for a computer. If this software has a faulty code, it will not function properly. Sometimes fixing a single letter, number or symbol is all it takes to solve the problem. I call it the "missing piece." The same applies for us. By fixing, replacing or rearranging certain beliefs and identifying our missing piece, we can completely transform our life. As humans, it's in our nature to seek this missing piece, that aspect of our lives we feel is missing. It could be mental (such as knowledge, insight, wisdom, or strategy), or it could be physical (health) or emotional (such as a partner, love and support) or a better job. Whatever it is you feel is missing from your life. you can achieve it by applying the tools presented in this book.

This system will bring your attention to deeper understandings of how things work in life and elevate your consciousness to a much higher level of awareness. These strategies will help you find your missing piece and utilize it to open the flood gates of health, happiness, and prosperity into your life.

The Trouble with Goals

Most authors and seminar presenters talk about goals. It's drilled into our heads about how important they are and that we need to have them to succeed. I get it and I completely agree, but often when people think of or hear the word "goal" they unconsciously associate it with a failure from their past, which sets them up for failure before they even start.

When we write or declare our goals to ourselves or others—whether it's to lose weight, go to the gym and get in shape, or start a new habit or a new year's resolution—we rarely accomplish them. When we don't, there is a negative association on a subconscious level with the idea of goal setting. It is then we become what I call "subconsciously damaged," a frame of mind which triggers a continuous cycle of negative thoughts and feelings toward our goals. *The good news is this cycle can be broken*, and that's what this system is all about. It changed my life, and it can change yours too!

You might be asking yourself, *how is it I haven't heard about this powerful information before?* The answer is simple: no one has ever exposed it to you.

Let's start with your parents. They were your first teachers in life. They taught you the things they had been taught and what they knew—nothing more, nothing less. They didn't intend to misguide you. Just like many of us, they themselves were not aware of their own inner power. Then, when you went to school, you were not taught the basic principles behind how to harness the power of your mind, because your teachers most likely didn't know them either.

Wouldn't it be great if we could learn how our minds and bodies work together to create and design our lives? We spend so many years and so much money on education, yet we don't take one single course on how to become the best versions of ourselves or even learn how to tap into our internal powers when our minds and bodies work together in harmony.

I created this system to keep you continually connected to the powers of your mental and physical energy. It will boost your awareness level and help you break through the barriers now keeping you from achieving the things you want in your life. As you read, take notes and highlight the things which trigger something for you. It is important for you to take the necessary actions when you read the book. Taking notes and highlighting the words resonating with you will help you to begin the action necessary to embody the Prosperity System and reach the results you desire.

I believe you are going to absolutely love the mind-power techniques in this book. This information is directed at you. Yes, YOU. Not necessarily at your relationships or your golf game or your business or anything else, but at YOU. As we increase our understanding and awareness of how we function as humans in mind, body, and spirit, you will start to see how everything around you will start to shift and change.

This system will teach you the rules and laws of the mind and provide two critical sets of tools to help you shift your perceptions and beliefs. There is a specific process to get your good energy flowing by doing the right things in the right order and at the right time. You will get more clarity on this in the chapters which address the mind-power techniques and the four stages of transformation.

This book is not written to be a one-time pep talk like many other self-help books on the market today. Even more important, it is also not just a "positive thinking" book that tries to paint over and cover up negative beliefs, which at best will provide results that are temporary and evaporate overnight. This book is different. It is a practical and intentional thinking model based on understanding and awareness. It is about taking massive action. It is a way of living. It is a system to be used to transform your life by changing your programming (belief system). It is explained in simple, plain language, and is formatted in a fun and easy way for you to achieve the greatness you deserve.

The Prosperity System is a systematic practice, not just a philosophy. For example, if we asked ten people to bake a carrot cake, and we provided each of them with a detailed recipe and the required ingredients. All of the cakes would be different. Statistically 4-5 people will bake a cake that is below average, 3-4 will be average, and 2 will be excellent. The two who did a great job likely followed the recipe accurately and had certain awareness to the process. They had an idea, a mindset and an expectation of how their carrot cake would *taste, look, and feel*. They accomplished excellence by doing things in a *certain way, in a certain "energy" with a certain "expectation"* and they did it in the *right order* of adding the ingredients together at the *right time* to bake the cake. That's exactly how it is in life.

We need the right mindset energy when it comes to achieving goals! We need to have the right expectations and do things in the right order at the right time!

Why I Want You to Succeed

When I was a young boy, I felt God asked me certain questions. He asked, *"Nabil, what do you want to become when you grow up? What contribution do you want to make to the world? How are you going to serve, and live your calling and purpose?"*

My answer is simply *"I want to teach, inspire, and help people to become aware of their Divine power within. I want to connect the seekers to their hidden powers and teach them how they can use it to build prosperity in their lives."*

God seemed to humor me and said, *"OK. You got it! But first you must be tested. I will put you through a series of ups and downs,*

22

heartaches, pain, confusion, and depression. I will challenge you so you can learn, discover, and gain valuable experiences to unlock the door to understand life well enough to grow, teach and inspire others to discover their own hidden powers and to open their minds and hearts to prosperity."

The truth is the challenges, struggles, and lessons are what really transforms a person. That's what builds character and understanding. Struggling is part of succeeding. Losing is part of gaining and winning. If we do not encounter difficult times or challenges at various points in our lives, we are not growing. When we can learn from life's lessons, we gain strength and have the ability and capacity to deal with almost anything that comes our way. On the flip side, if we choose to ignore those lessons, we fall victim to having to repeat them repeatedly. For me, my life's lessons taught me two things:

1. We are the cause of everything that happens to us in our lives. We create our own reality—and we have the power to control it if we choose.
2. The "so-called" missing piece is alive and living within us. We must become aware of its existence and know how to harness it!

After this self-realization and understanding, my wife and I started practicing and applying The Prosperity System. We were able to alter and shift our consciousness from a victim mentality to one which enabled us to re-connect with our Divine inner powers and reprogram our belief system which controls our lives. By using these techniques, we shifted our belief systems into one that fostered our new purpose, vision and goals. We quickly began to see our mindset begin to shift and things started to happen. My entrepreneurial spirit began to soar again, I was back to making deals on different projects. I was back to finding joy in what I did. And, slowly, but surely, I rebuilt a life of style and adventure.

Most people who struggle financially have a psychological blockage about prosperity and what it means. I have been there myself. Please understand, the forces and the energies that ignite and activate your mind and heart to be open to prosperity are both mental and spiritual. It is important to have a balance of both. Once you begin to study, understand, and apply the mental mind-power techniques and spiritual laws for prosperity, you will become aware you are not trying to force God or the universe or any other source to provide you with anything. Since we are *ONE* with God, the abundance of prosperity is ours already.

God is the source of our prosperity, not other people or circumstances. People are the channels that show up in our life to assist us to get what we want, but when they show up to help us, they show up with their own unique (programming) belief system too. We are all born without programming. As we go through life, our programming (mindset) is filled with information and ideas—sometimes good, and sometimes not so good. Some programming comes from our own experiences, while others are instilled in us by others.

Most of the time, we are unaware of this subconscious programming and don't have a say in how our beliefs and mindsets are programmed. It's important to know and be aware of this fact, and even more importantly, you must understand you don't have to live with this programming forever. You have the power to change it!

The Prosperity System

This system has evolved and developed slowly over several years but is the very system I used and still use to transform my life. By training my mind to think thoughts of opportunity rather than fear, solutions rather than problems, positivity rather than negativity, I began to operate on a plane of possibility where everything I wanted already existed. It was mine for the taking. All I had to do was visualize it in my mind, feel it in my heart and take the physical actions toward achieving it.

In this state, we can begin to understand the power of the conscious and subconscious mind. The conscious mind is where our thoughts are rationalized, quantified, and analyzed. We absorb and collect thoughts and ideas we have learned or have been told. It's the conscious mind that tells us, *don't touch the fire. It's hot and it will burn you.* It's also the part of the mind that instills fear, worry, and doubt. The subconscious mind, on the other hand, is where our secret, hidden power lies. The subconscious mind can't differentiate between what exists and what does not; what is real and what is an illusion. In the world of the subconscious mind, everything is true—and yet nothing is true. There is no concept of time. The subconscious is nothing but a series of NOW moments, which we will talk more about in a later chapter.

Understanding the foundation of the conscious and subconscious minds allow us to apply various mind-power techniques to alter and shift them. These proven techniques will systematically instill new empowering beliefs affecting the way you think (mindset), and ultimately result in the manifestation of your desires.

I have been an entrepreneur all my life and have created many businesses over the years using this system. I've been successful with several ventures from real estate and land investments, to buying and selling businesses, conducting seminars around the world, and co-founding a cruise line. Much of this can be attributed to my work ethic and actions, but most of it is simply because I understand the levels of awareness and mind powers each one of us have within us.

Along my journey, I have been coached and mentored by amazing people and earned special certifications, and a reputation for my expertise. I have traveled across the United States sharing this knowledge. I was even selected to travel to

China alongside other influential businesspeople and politicians to explore, teach, train, coach, and mentor Chinese entrepreneurs. Though these were great experiences, none of these compared to the lessons I learned deep within myself. I was my most influential teacher — tapping my intuition and the understanding of how to access my secret, hidden power buried deep inside my subconscious mind.

Over the years, I have seen so many ordinary people successfully use and integrate this system to reach the success they desired. I know it will work for anyone willing and ready to open their minds and hearts to their prosperity (happiness, health or wealth). It is not for the faint of heart though. It does require work and a commitment. But it is for those who are ready to take action to make a true transformation.

The Prosperity System is centered around two main areas of focus:

MENTAL
(Consciousness)

PHYSICAL
(Action)

There is a third element too, your spiritual power. Throughout the contents of this book I will refer to a higher power—God, the universe, nature, or life force energy—and will use these terms interchangeably. Please understand I have respect for everyone's individual beliefs and understand there is no single right, or wrong belief. They simply are. Please use whatever description you have for your higher power when you read this book.

Another formula we will refer to is "what" plus "why" impacts the "how."

In any given situation or circumstance, there is a "what," or process of identification: *What is happening? What is the issue? What needs my attention? What preconceived ideas or biases do I have?* Once we have identified the situation, we move onto the "why," which is lodged in the conscious mind to rationalize the situation: *Why is this happening? Why do I feel this way? Why do I have these beliefs? Why can't I do this?*

Finally, we use the answers from these first two phases to identify the "how." This is where the real magic of "The Prosperity System" takes place. We will use the power of our mental and physical bodies to learn exactly "how" to create success.

The Journey Begins

It's time to shift your mindset so you can take the bold steps necessary to make your success a reality. This system is experiential learning with massive action. You can't just *read* the book. Think of when you purchased something functional such as a TV, phone, tablet, car, stereo, computer, or any device. You opened the box, reviewed an owner's manual that illustrated and explained the basic operations for the item in order to get the maximum benefits and the most efficient ways to use it. The interesting thing is, many of us will casually review or disregard the manual entirely. Instead, we will rely solely on our own experiences to operate the item and never really get the full functionality or maximum benefits of the device. There is a good reason for this behavior, and it relates back to our individual personalities. Some people like to have the full details and understand the mechanics of things from A-Z; they want to know everything. Others simply want to know the process without the mechanics and details. They have a *"just show me what to do, and I will do it"* mentality. In short, The Prosperity System is the owner manual to understand your own mind power. You must read it entirely to understand its full potential, but then you must take the actions in order to have the transformation you want.

It is only when you shift your mindset and re-connect to your Divine inner powers that your thoughts lead to better results: Thoughts influence behaviors...behaviors create experiences... experiences create emotions...emotions drive and influence our actions and results. Once you become aware of this chain reaction, you will learn how to control results and you will be off to the races!

CHAPTER THREE
God's Instructions

When God created the world, He called for a meeting with all of us and said:

"I am the creator. I am creating this world. I am creating a big story and I want you to be part of it. I want you to become a co-creator with Me. I want you to create your own story. You will be able to design your story of your own life in the privacy of your own mind. And you must learn how to design and create your world. Either on your own or all of you can work together.

In order to become a co-creator with Me, I am going to give you some of my Divine power to use. With this power, you can create anything you want. Do you see all that space (ether) all around you? It is not just empty space. It's my energy. It's intelligence and substance at the same time. You can extract from it anything you want. You can be whatever you want to be, do, or have. But it is also your responsibility to create the programming (belief system or paradigm) that runs and operates my Divine power in you to serve you and create the way you want things to be."

Everything in your life has a specific energy structure "signature." Your job is to "BE THAT ENERGY!" When you learn to match the energy of the things you want, and act towards it, you will attract and create anything you want.

God continued, *"I will provide you with two sets of tools:*

1. *The five senses: sight, sound, taste, touch, and smell.*
2. *The six mental faculties of the mind to help you control your paradigm (belief): imagination, will, memory, perception, intuition, and reason.*

Once you learn how to use the tools correctly, you will be able to control and design your life. Keep in mind you must learn how to use them within the constructs of the rules and the laws governing them. Learning to accurately use these tools can be very tricky, but very rewarding.

There are many ways to communicate with Me. You can contact Me and have access to Me with all the knowledge, wisdom and information you need to create and build your world any time you want. I will respond to you according to your demands. So, some of the communication with you will be in the form of intuition and instinct. I want you to become aware of them because this inner voice is MY VOICE to communicate with you, to give you guidance, insights, tips and hints.

Don't be ignorant about this powerful tool. Use it to your advantage. It is your instinctive power in life.

You can also communicate with Me and be as close to me as humanly possible when you are in the "NOW" moment. I live in the present moment! When you are in the NOW present moment you become: No-one, no-thing, no-body in no-time and no-space. You are away from all the noise and distractions. In this NOW moment, you are with Me and I am with you. So, if you want to find me, you have to tap into the NOW moment.

You can access being in the NOW moment in a lot of different ways, and you can learn them on your own or with the help of others. One of the tools I will give you is a very powerful energy (sex energy) to enjoy and conceive offspring. But that is not all you can use it for. This energy is so powerful you can use it to extract and carve your own reality of health, happiness, relationships, and wealth too! You can create anything you want in an expedited supercharged way. It has velocity and speed. Study it, learn it, and use it.

You will have a special direct link with Me. Your direct line to communicate with Me is being in the present (NOW moment). When you are in this state of being, you have my attention and you become a co-creator with Me.

I ask you to do yourself a favor during your life journey on planet Earth: BE GRATEFUL AND THANKFUL TO MY DIVINE POWER IN YOU!

Remember this: gratitude is one of the most powerful emotions to boost your level of achieving. When you are grateful, the mind and the body are in the state of being where your goals have already been met. You will feel an "it's been achieved" feeling. This is important. When you become aware of this power, everything in your life will flow effortlessly. But you must work for it. It is the mental work required on your part to create the life you want.

I AM gifting you some of my Divine power for you to enjoy. However, it is no fun to give you my Divine power and make it easy for you to find and access it. That's why I refer to it as your "secret" hidden power. You must discover it for yourself.

Let's make it an exciting and fun journey."

Then, God asked all of us, *"Where should I hide my Divine power (the power of the subconscious) from you?"* Some of us suggested hiding it on the top of the mountain. He replied, *"No, that would be too easy to find. You will learn to climb mountains."* Others suggested to hide it at the bottom of the ocean, to which He said, *"No, you will learn how to swim and scuba dive."* Finally, He said, *"I know where to hide it where you will have a hard time finding and discovering it. I will hide it within each of you."*

So that's what He did. He "hid" this Divine power inside each of us. It is our secret, hidden power. It is the missing piece of our existence which we are constantly yearning to find. Most of us look outside ourselves to find it, but in truth it's intimately closer than we think. The sad part about this is most people will go through their entire lives not knowing how to discover or use their own secret power. They never realize the missing piece or "Divine power" was inside them all along!

God had one additional fundamental insight to share...

> *"Before I allow you to begin co-creating with Me and each other, I will share with you what to do in order to save time and energy to get everything you want in life.*
>
> *Your priority should always be to focus your energy to serve others. That's what helps you stay connected with your inner Divine power, which is MY POWER. If you feel helpless, stuck, and unfulfilled, it is because you have disconnected your power temporarily. And the reason this happened is because you focused only on yourself and no one else.*

Service and helping each other is key to staying connected and getting what you want. There will be people who will show up in your life to help you re-connect. It's just part of the journey to learn and grow, and it makes life fun. Relax. It will always work out in the end. Everything happens for a reason.

The Three Stages of Life

As part of our journey through this life, we will go through three stages of life: childhood, adulthood, and transformation. God explains...

> *"When you first enter this world as a human on Earth, you will be equipped with your mind, body, and spirit, but it will be a new beginning. You will forget everything you once knew about yourself the minute you arrive. It will seem as if your memory has been erased. As a baby and through your early years of childhood, it will be a fresh start where you will begin a new journey toward discovery. Over time during adulthood, you will start gaining awareness of your own spirit and oneness with it. The true, and final stage will be a period of transformation where you will become aware of your oneness with Me!"*

First Stage: Childhood

Childhood is the entry point into life and will last several years into adolescence. At this stage, you are highly connected with your inner power, but you are not aware of it. As you grow, you will begin to use some of the tools, such as imagination, which is both powerful and fun. During this stage, your conscious mind is in an "OFF" position. It gets activated and slowly switches "ON" as you grow older. At times, you may feel helpless, but your powerful subconscious mind is working for you. You are like a sponge learning everything around you. However, very soon your subconscious mind will be fed with information (programming, beliefs) by others from your environment. Some of it will be good and some of it is not. Most of the programming in your subconscious mind happens before you're 7-8 years old!

Second Stage: Adulthood

You could arrive into adulthood as either connected or temporarily disconnected from your inner power. The good news is your conscious mind is in the "ON" position and you have a choice in controlling who you are and how you want things to be. During your adulthood you may or may not identify with some of the programming you acquired. You may hear the voices and past programming of your parents, schoolteachers, or family members echoing within you. Remember, regardless of your programming until this point, those who nurtured and guided you during childhood, did so in your best interest. If it was misguided, they didn't know any better. They were never taught or had an awareness of how to transform their lives. You should not blame them for any of the programming. This will only hurt you by pushing you further towards a "victim mentality." You will learn the techniques to change this programming in this book!

Third Stage: Transformation

Transformation occurs when you become aware there is a Divine power inside you and understand it's always been available to you. This is the truest stage of existence. It becomes clear you don't need to change how you feel about your past to create your future. All you must do is visualize your future and associate it with the corresponding feelings and emotions. Just let go of the past and live in the NOW to create your future. Transformation is when you learn how to bring the invented future into the NOW. Achieving transformation is a big step—many never even discover it at all! No matter how old you are when you discover it, be grateful and don't beat yourself up for not discovering it earlier. You, like all of us, just got busy and consumed by all the distractions and challenges in life. Take hold of this new discovery and make the most of it.

Remember the conscious mind is designed to deal with the past and the future. Most people will get a little confused. They will get stuck in either reliving the past or trying so hard to live in the future they forget about the present moment—the NOW—where God lives.

You will learn the future gets created in the NOW. The future is filled with NOW moments. As you connect in the NOW, you create the life you want, but we humans call it the "future."

God wants you to be prosperous in every way possible. It's His desire for you to be rich in life so He can work through you. If you have the best life has to offer, you can extend your prosperity to others. So yes, strive for richness in life so you can co-create the future for humanity.

Whether you are rich or poor, don't forget to give a portion of what you earn to help the disadvantaged, because that's how God is able to open the floodgates of prosperity in your life. The act of giving will dissolve any blockages inhibiting you from inheriting a life of abundance.

I always love sharing this insight and I use it as part of my teachings. It is the foundation of our training and I will bring parts of it back to your attention as we go through the process of learning the mind-power techniques for transformation.

As you make your journey through the three stages, it is important to understand your dream or vision in order to make the jump from Adulthood to the Transformation stage. There are two things you must know before you can begin to manifest prosperity or anything else in your life. You must know them and understand them very well:
1. You must know **where you are**
2. You must know **where you are going**

Simple, right? Then, why are so many people stuck in their lives—losing their health, homes, jobs, and fortunes? Why do so many give up on their dreams? The answer is something called the "**PARADIGM**."

The paradigm is our belief system, or "structured energy," we use to create our realities. It is a culmination of the beliefs and habits which have been engrained into our subconscious minds—whether they are right or wrong—in the form of brain cells of recognition. They are the structured energy in us that drives and controls us in every aspect of our lives. I will explain this paradigm and its importance, including how we must learn to control it in the upcoming chapters.

Keep in mind the body's energy and the mind's power energy are connected and one. They feed into each other. Pay close attention to your body. You need a healthy body to accomplish what you want in life and to enjoy life.

Preparing for Prosperity

As you begin your journey toward prosperity, please understand you are not alone in this journey. We are all travelers on a journey. We all encounter intersections and make several turns in order to get to our destination. At different mile markers we encounter people, events, opportunities, and life forces which lead us to new intersections where we must make choices. Sometimes, we meet others who are at the same crossroad who inspire, complement, and enhance our lives. It is in this powerful convergence of ideas, visions, and energies where we unite to help and serve each other on our paths to prosperity.

Though at times you may fear taking certain paths. The Prosperity System is designed to be your roadmap to guide you down the path that's right for you. Remember, no path is right or wrong; every decision simply IS. What's important is it's right for YOU at that time. When we have this level of awareness of the Divine power within us, the people, circumstances, events, forces, and incidents will show up to light your path and open doors for you.

Before you start reading the remaining chapters of this book, I would like to ask three things of you:

1. **Be open-minded to the information contained here.**
   It does not contradict any religion or culture and if

there is a part you don't understand, it's OK. Just don't reject it. You will understand it as you become more aware. Be open-minded and allow the information, concepts, and ideas to sink in.

2. **Get clear on your goal, project, or vision.** This should be something you really want. Your objective in reading this book is to get new ideas and an awareness to help you get what you want. Follow me throughout this system and journal your thoughts—take notes as you get ideas. I will show you how to get what you want. How to do the "HOW." Not just what needs to be done. But *how* to do it and take massive action towards your goals.

3. **Don't read the Appendix's at the end of the book until you finish reading the whole book.** By the time you finish reading this book, you will have a much higher level of awareness and understanding on how to use the tools, the laws of the mind, and the mind-power techniques.

It's never too late to accomplish and live the life you desire. The secret is within you, and it's time to discover it.

CHAPTER FOUR
Designing Your Prosperous Life

"Life isn't about finding yourself. Life is about creating yourself."
George Bernard Shaw

We are responsible for creating our own reality, whether we are doing it consciously or unconsciously. We are the cause of everything we experience. As you read and apply the mind-power techniques, you will come to better understand this, and will discover the power of this concept—it's all about your mindset!

We all want prosperity. So why aren't we all prosperous?

Most people want to start their own business (or a new career) and prosper for all the right reasons. But sadly, about 90 percent will go out of business within five years or less. If you take two people with the exact same credentials and conditions to start a business, one may do very well, and the other likely will be out of business in no time. Why the different outcomes?

The reason is mindset. One has success in mind, and the other is afraid of success, or has a failure mindset. These failed businesses and bankruptcies are people with faces, names, voices, kids, families, and unfulfilled dreams. These are real people who want prosperity in their lives but are not in the right frame of mind.

I believe together we can reduce or prevent business failure statistics if these entrepreneurs become aware of their Divine power and the importance of having the right mindset. In order to create the right mindset for success, we must first know ourselves, our creative faculties and how to use them correctly.

We must:
- ✓ Know the rules and the universal laws governing us
- ✓ Work with the power within us and not against it
- ✓ Learn how to be creators and not competitors
- ✓ Engage in a mindset-reboot and reset process on a regular basis

Ask yourself, *what kind of person do I need to become in order to succeed and achieve my goals?* In order to become that person, you must think, feel, and act as the person you want to become. You must *"be that energy!"*

"Self-confidence is the first requisite to great undertaking."
–Samuel Johnson

My intention is to train you to create habits that serve and support your goals. To do this, you must have the right foundation of beliefs to support where you are going. With this understanding, you can then begin to master and train your mind to accomplish what you want in life and business. I believe the path to freedom begins with your confidence level and the energy level at which it vibrates.

When we have confidence in ourselves, people will trust us more, which brings more referrals, more business, and more money. Confidence is key. No one wants to do business or pay attention to a person who isn't confident in themselves or what they are doing.

"If I lose confidence in myself, I have the Universe against me."
–Ralph Waldo Emerson

Where do we find confidence? Can we find it in the physical world? The answer is *NO!* You can't go to the supermarket and buy confidence. It can't be transferred or inherited. The only way to find it is to develop it—and you can! It all starts from within. It is only when you learn to control your inner world you can begin to control the outer world. This is one of the first laws of the mind.

Confidence has its own vibration of energy, just like everything else that exists. In order to be and have confidence, you must become the energy of confidence which leads to the lifestyle you want. Ultimately, you either actively design your life through consciousness, or passively allow it to be shaped by the realities of others or the environment. The choice is yours and yours alone.

Being a conscious architect of your reality is not easy, but you can train your mind to do it. It takes effort, and a strong discipline to practice the mind-power techniques. Don't get frustrated and give up. The worst thing you can do is place the blame elsewhere; on other people, conditions, timing, etc. You must take ownership and responsibility for your reality in order to alter your paradigm, or belief system. Why? Because our paradigm is what controls our thoughts and actions. For us to have power over our paradigm, we must understand everything about it—the language it speaks, the medium in which it communicates, and how it affects the mind and body. Studying and understanding the mind must be a top priority to be able to live life to the fullest.

> *"Mind is the master power that molds and makes,*
> *and we are mind, and evermore we take*
> *the tool of thought, and shaping what we will.*
> *Bring forth a thousand joys, a thousand ills,*
> *we think in secret, and it comes to pass —*
> *Our world is but our looking glass."*
> —James Allen

Our mind is a precious gift. It's what differentiates us from every other creature on this planet. The more we understand and use it, the better results we will have. By understanding how the mind works, it gives us a measurable level of confidence, and most importantly, the ability to believe in our mind. It has infinite power to create. If we know what we want, our mind can help us attract the energies to manifest it.

You Are What You Think
What do you want most to happen in your life?

If you and I were to go out on the street and stop 100 people and ask every one of them what they really wanted in life and in business (i.e. their goals), most of them probably wouldn't be able to tell us. Most people don't know what they want. Most of their answers will be very vague. They would likely give us general answers such as "I want to be happy," "I want to be wealthy," or "I want to travel the world." In fact, only about 3% of the population know what they want and how to accomplish it.

The reason people do not have the things they say they want is simple. They
1) don't have a vivid image of what they want.
2) have not been taught how to use their desires as fuel to initiate their ability to manifest.
3) do not speak the words of their desire in the NOW. They say it as if it will happen "someday," which is actually a code for "never." With this mindset, they get frustrated by wasting time and energy and often stop trying.

On the flip side, if we asked the same 100 people what they *"DON'T"* want, almost all of them would be able to give us the specific things they are thinking every day. Their answers will likely be "I don't want to be poor," "I don't want to gain weight," "I don't want to live in fear," or "I don't want to be alone." When this becomes their focus, that's exactly what they attract!

Acting the Part of What You Want

One of the reasons we all love to go to the movies is to escape our own realities and jump into someone else's life. For me, I love to see Al Pacino, Harrison Ford, or Sharon Stone let go of their true identities and embody their character in the story. As it is with great actors, they allow themselves to be completely consumed by the essence, "or energy," of their character.

Energy is everything. It is everything you see, taste, touch, hear, and think. Energy presents itself as either invisible waves or visible particles. Nothing in this universe is ever created or destroyed. Think about it—everything we want in life is, in some capacity, already here!

By this notion, if you know who or what you want to become, it's simple: you "*act the part.*" You let go of your perceived existence, bring your mind into the NOW, and reach out with your mind to tap into the eternal energy—energy that has the potential to transform into anything you desire with the help of your consciousness. If your vision is strong, and you are intimately connected to your inner Divine power of the NOW, you can cause that energy to organize into matter with your thoughts, feelings and beliefs. It really is that simple, but it's not easy at first. It requires knowledge, awareness, and practice. But, after a while, it can become second nature.

If you're having a hard time accepting and understanding this concept, think about the discovery of how someone made an airplane fly. The laws of physics and aerodynamics always existed, but it took the awareness—and the idea—of how to apply them to fly an airplane. An airplane didn't simply manifest itself; it was potential energy that transformed into an idea inside the minds of the Wright brothers. And that applies to everything we have discovered or are about to discover. Awareness brings it to life.

In doing this ourselves, we must become aware of what we want, and bring our full attention into the NOW. On a spiritual level, this is commonly called "mindfulness," but on a physiological level, what we are doing is aligning our true essence with the structured energy cells in our brain. In short, this is where our minds and bodies work as one to initiate the transformation of shapeless energy into physical energy. When these two energies converge, our minds create the thoughts and emotions, and our bodies perform the action. These thoughts and actions exude their own frequencies of energy to attract other energies of the same vibration. When we do this, we are both attracting and emanating energies to manifest the thoughts and ideas of our mindset—whether it is positive or negative. Within the construct of the laws of the mind and the universe, we are constantly creating, both consciously and unconsciously. The results of our creations are simply a reflection of our awareness and understanding of how to tap into our personal source of energy.

So, here's the billion-dollar question: *"How do you grow and expand your level of awareness to manifest what you want?"*

It can be done through:
- ✓ Effective education to elevate your level of awareness of the powerful being you are as a creator
- ✓ Specialized knowledge of how your mind works and how to apply the mind-power techniques
- ✓ Self-realization of how powerful your thought forces are in creating and manifesting — all the time
- ✓ Having the right coaches and mentors in your life to help guide you toward a higher level of awareness

What's Causing Disease?

Over the years, I became aware of a holistic doctor, Dr. Fleet from San Antonio, Texas who had been involved in the healing arts since 1934. This brilliant and extraordinary man and doctor once stated, "We are treating the symptoms, the effects, and the disease, but we are not treating the cause. So, what's

43

causing disease?" Dr. Fleet continued, "The source of the problem is just expressing itself through pain and dysfunction in the body. The real cause is found in the mind."

Dr. Fleet knew in order to heal the body, we must have a picture of health in the mind. There is just one problem; while doctors have seen pictures of the brain, no one has ever seen the mind!

What Does Your Mind Look Like?
Take a couple of minutes to think about this question. How do we even begin to answer it? Imagine you and I are sitting across from one another and I ask you to think of your car. What happened? Did a picture of your car pop up on the screen of your mind? How did this happen?

Here's why that happened. When I said, "think of your car," I activated my vocal cords and made a sound which is a light wave frequency. This frequency vibrated through time and space and was picked up by your hearing senses, which activated structured energy (cells of recognition) in your brain. These structured energy cells released a signal of recognition to your brain. You associated with your perception of your car; and boom, the image appeared in your mind.

Words trigger pictures and images. Think of your dog, boat, front door, or even your kitchen sink. As soon as you read or hear these words, pictures will appear on the big screen of your mind. We communicate through sounds, or vibrational energy patterns—each of which have pictures, images and feelings associated with them.

When we try to communicate with someone in a language we don't understand, we hear sounds that don't correlate to any cells of recognition in our brain. There is no structured energy. In fact, the way we learn a language is by programming new cells of recognition through repetitive sounds, pictures, and feelings.

44

Now, think back to when I asked you what your mind looks like. What happened? Most people draw a blank or resort to an image of a brain. Your brain is an amazing, magnificent, and powerful organ, but it is not your mind. The brain is simply an instrument of the mind—a tool to alter energetic vibrations.

Vibration is what we call feelings on the conscious level. If someone asked you, "How are you feeling today?" You might say, "Not good." You don't say, "I am in a bad vibration of energy today." When you are feeling bad, it's likely because you have been thinking bad thoughts and ideas, and visualizing dark, dreary, and negative mental images. This negativity converts into an equivalent chemical reaction, which we associate with a feeling—in this case, "not good."

To change your feelings, you need to change your vibration. To feel good, you must start with thinking and visualizing, or remembering the sensation of something good. As this vibrational energy begins to take over, you will start to feel more rested, relaxed, and focused. You will feel calmer, more energetic, and at ease. These sensations become your energy.

The key is while we all think in pictures and images, we cannot imagine what the mind looks like because it is an "activity"— not a "thing." Therefore, no one has a clear picture of the mind. If there is no picture, there is confusion. If there is confusion on the inside, there will also be confusion on the outside.

A Picture of the Mind

I have been a student of the mind for over thirty years and have read many books, attended multiple seminars, and studied with great mentors. I want to share with you the following diagram and graphic representation of our mind, created by Dr. Fleet in 1934.

Diagram 1 is an interpretation of a "Universal Mind." While everyone has their own perception of what the mind might look like, the following graphics suggests all conscious minds have the same structure which contain both the mind and body.

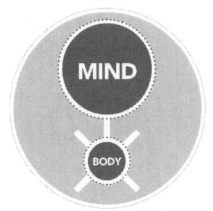

Diagram 1

This picture of the mind and body was introduced in 1934 by the founder of Concept Therapy — Dr. Fleet from San Antonio, Texas.

In Diagram 2, you will notice there is a separation line between the conscious and the subconscious mind. It is one mind with two chambers—like the color chambers of a rainbow. There are seven colors of the rainbow, with no real separation between them. They are just different vibrations of a single rainbow.

Diagram 2

In Diagram 3, we see in addition to our mind, we have been gifted with five senses. We can see, hear, smell, taste, and touch. As you'll remember in Chapter 3, these are the first set of tools God gifted us. These five senses were designed for our protection and safety, to help us communicate with others, and to evaluate and decipher incoming information from the outer world.

Diagram 3
The Five Senses

In Diagram 4, we take a closer look at the conscious mind, which is also known as "the thinking mind." This is the part of the mind we use to communicate with each other and form ideas and concepts. The thinking mind uses data from past experiences, expected outcomes, and our existing belief systems to make choices. It is here where we are able to accept or reject an idea or choose a plan of action. The thoughts that surface in our conscious mind influence the results we get in life.

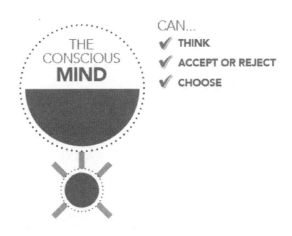

CAN...
- ✔ THINK
- ✔ ACCEPT OR REJECT
- ✔ CHOOSE

Diagram 4
The Thinking Mind

Moving onto Diagram 5, we dive deeper into the subconscious mind, which is where your secret, hidden power lies. Unlike the conscious mind, it does not have the capability to reject a thought or idea, nor does it differentiate between what is real and what is just imagined. It is also the part of the mind that expresses itself through feelings (vibration of energy). Feelings evoke emotions, which are carried out in the body as a physical action.

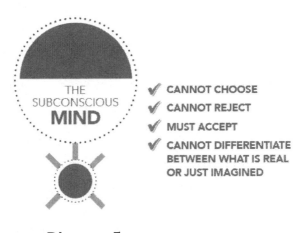

- ✔ CANNOT CHOOSE
- ✔ CANNOT REJECT
- ✔ MUST ACCEPT
- ✔ CANNOT DIFFERENTIATE BETWEEN WHAT IS REAL OR JUST IMAGINED

Diagram 5
The Subconscious Mind

The body is the instrument that carries out the emotions and thoughts of the mind. It is the physical vessel that places one foot in front of the other toward our destiny. It is also important to understand that the body's actions and emotions impact the mind. We must take care of our physical bodies to facilitate the maximum production of energy. Without it, our path to prosperity will be slowed, if not halted. On the flip side, there is nothing more powerful than when the mind and the body are aligned and working together. When this happens, your path to prosperity is on the fast track!

Finally, do you remember our conversation with God where we learned about the two sets of tools? Diagram 6 highlights the six mental faculties of the mind that make up the second set of tools designed to change and shift our paradigm, or belief system: imagination, will, reason, memory, perception, and intuition. When you take charge of your paradigm, your life will change. Just like that!

Your paradigm is nothing more than your perception of who you *"think"* you are. It drives how you think, act, feel, and most importantly how you make decisions. Your first step in true transformation is becoming aware you have a choice in every NOW moment. The choices you make may be based on what you've been taught to believe by others. But the only person who truly has ANY control of your next step is YOU. When you question, challenge and let go of everything you thought you once knew, you can recreate your sense of who you are, how you think, what you want to do, and how you want to do it. These tools are the anchor points in which you begin to question your current paradigm, and then take actionable steps towards controlling your life.

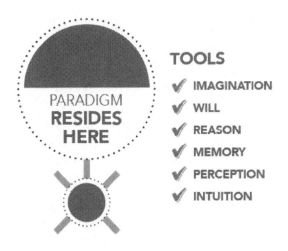

Diagram 6

The six mental faculties of the mind that make up the second set of tools designed to change and shift your paradigm

CHAPTER FIVE
Knowing Yourself

"It only takes one person to change your life—YOU."
Ruth Casey

It only takes one person to truly transform your life across all aspects, and that person is YOU!

Have you ever wondered who you really are? We all have. It's an innate yearning to constantly seek out who we really are so we can become whole.

Who Are You?

In becoming whole, you must first understand *who* you are. Throughout history, you will find the adage, "know thyself." It is a wise statement which holds more power than most people understand. To know yourself is to know who you truly are in this marvelous universe, the role you play within it, and the true inner power you possess.

But, what does it really mean to know yourself? Since birth, we have come to know our name, where we live, our strengths and weaknesses, and what foods we like—but those are just labels we use to describe ourselves. What most people don't know enough about is who they are in the context of their mind, body, and soul—more specifically, how they function together and interact with universal existence (life force energy).

You must take care to nurture both your mind and physical body during the process of learning your true self. The mind feeds on thoughts that require energy, which is a product of the body. If your body isn't healthy, it's hard to get your mind to work optimally.

Knowing yourself means aligning your mind, body, and soul. It is only in knowing yourself that you understand the mind and body are one and are infinitely connected. To know yourself is to recognize and claim the full potential and power in you, and in all of humanity. It is embodying your truest nature; being satisfied in your thoughts without judgement; acknowledging your feelings and releasing your emotions without hesitation; and acting confidently without fear. Knowing yourself not only impacts your own life, but the lives of others who surround you. This realization is the ultimate secret power!

One of the first steps in learning to know ourselves is cultivating a healthy relationship between our mind, body, and soul. This can be translated into three key relationships with:

1. Ourselves
2. Others
3. The Universe

The most important relationship is the one we have with ourselves. We must be in harmony and fully understand *"who"* we are. An old Egyptian proverb states, "Know yourself and you will possess the keys to the universe and the secrets of the gods."

Of course, understanding our oneness with the Creator and how our mind works gives us immediate confidence and power in everything we do. Confidence within is key! Emerson said it beautifully, *"If I have lost confidence in myself, I have the Universe against me."*

Designing Who You Want to Become

Knowing yourselves is one thing but getting yourself into the right action by fulfilling your role is another—and far more important. We are not here just to know ourselves; we are here to design and create ourselves.

Diagram 7 is a roadmap of how we can become our own conscious design engineers. Take your time to study, learn, and imprint it into your consciousness. Once you do this and begin to use it correctly, your life will change forever.

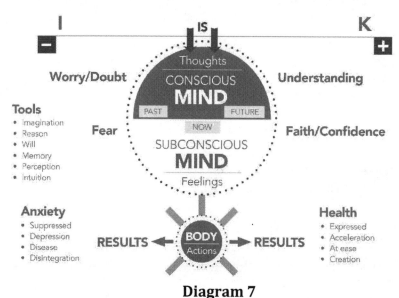

Diagram 7
The roadmap to become conscious design engineers.

In the previous diagrams, we dissected the individual components of Diagram 7, including how the mind is divided into the conscious mind, where thoughts are born, and the sub-conscious mind, where our feelings are created. The mind and body are intimately connected, and the body is the vessel in which the mind carries out actions. We also discussed the six mental faculties of the mind which are illustrated along the left side of the diagram: imagination, reason, will, memory, perception, and intuition. Now, let's take a closer look into each of these components to understand the rest of the diagram.

The Conscious Mind

The conscious mind can perceive, judge, reason, accept, and reject thoughts. By its operation, we are aware of our power to think, will, know, and choose. Through our conscious mind, we have conscious communication with every part of our body. It is also responsible for gathering, analyzing and responding to the five senses of smell, taste, feeling, sound, and sight. Moreover, it can make decisions which create and shape our destiny.

This part of the mind is always thinking thoughts and forming ideas. It's like a machine without an *"OFF"* switch—constantly working and endlessly processing thoughts. Some of them are meaningless. Most of the time, those thoughts are controlled by what I call "the mind trickster." It's the analytical and critical part of the mind that insists we run things the way it deems necessary, rather than the way our true self wants. This, without a doubt, creates internal conflict.

If you want to make things happen in your life, you must identify the root of the thoughts coming from your conscious mind. Where are they coming from? Why are you thinking them? By doing this, you are bringing awareness to your thought process. If you can identify them, you can begin to address and restructure them into ones laden with confidence, happiness, success, prosperity, and abundance. In doing so, you are writing and designing the blueprints of your new consciousness.

While the conscious mind is indeed powerful, it cannot go anywhere in life without the cooperation of the subconscious mind. As a result, it must conform to be a co-creator alongside the subconscious mind.

The Subconscious Mind

The key to the subconscious mind is not just to know about it, but to experience the power found within it. The subconscious mind does not think, judge, reason, or reject. It simply accepts **all** the suggestions provided by the conscious mind.

This is where the power lies. It is also where your belief system (paradigm) resides which ultimately affects the things you do and why you do them. The conscious mind has the power to imprint a new paradigm through the subconscious mind using mind-power techniques. If repeated enough, the subconscious mind will begin to accept it, and once that happens, it sends a signal to the rest of the body so we can physically implement and experience our *new paradigm.*

The subconscious mind can't tell the difference between what is imagined and what is real!

This is true whether expressed in pictures or feelings and is an empowering piece of information. As you start applying what you are learning, you will get excited every time you experience this concept in action.

To give this idea some sort of framework, imagine you are watching a movie with some sad scenes. As you watch it, you get very emotionally involved and find yourself in tears. On a conscious level you know this is nothing more than a movie with actors acting out a scene, but you still cried. Why? This is an example of your subconscious mind reacting to a situation it cannot differentiate between what is real and what is imagined.

When we first learn about the subconscious mind's inability to tell the difference between what is imagined and what is real, we may wonder if it is a deficiency on the part of the subconscious mind. I can tell you it is not. It has been perfectly designed this way to serve us. This part of the mind controls and orchestrates all the involuntary functions of our body, such as breathing, digestion, blood circulation, elimination, reparation, and cell regeneration. It automates every operation within the body whether we are awake or asleep. More specifically, it has three primary functions:

1. To run our body's biochemical operating system
2. To act as the center for the programming of our software (paradigm, belief system)
3. To connect us with the universal subconscious mind (life force energy)

The subconscious mind is also the center of emotions and feelings. It's the storage for memory, beliefs, intuitions, and habits, and its actions are automatic in nature. Through it we are connected to the universal subconscious mind (life force energy).

The subconscious mind is the transportation medium to carry out our demands (paradigms, feelings, energy) of the way we want to live our lives. It's the vehicle and delivery system that connects us to the universal life force energy.

What's fascinating about the subconscious mind is its ability to connect to a collective consciousness. The collective subconscious mind is like the ocean. The ocean is a huge body of water and a very powerful force. When we scoop a small cup of water from the ocean, it is the same water with the same structure, but it is not as powerful as the whole ocean. Having said that, you and I, and the other seven billion people on planet earth, are like the cups of water taken from the ocean of collective consciousness (life force energy). That is exactly how it is with our subconscious mind. The whole ocean is contained within each cup; we must learn how to tap into the Divine power of the whole.

This subconscious powerhouse has phenomenal unlimited power that ultimately expresses itself through feelings and actions. As William James said, *"The power to move the world is in your subconscious mind."*

The Body is the Temple

The body is the physical representation of us, and therefore, the instrument of the mind. It is the house in which we live. It would **rather feel than think, but it influences how we think.** The body is directly connected with the universal life force energy.

Strictly from a biological standpoint, the body must have adequate production of energy to effectively perform all the functions it needs to do. The cells energy is ATP (Adenosine Triphosphate) and is produced within the mitochondria of each individual cell. For ATP to be produced, our cells need to be provided with oxygen and nutrients. Once these vital ingredients have been delivered to the cells via the bloodstream, ATP energy is enhanced forming healthy cells, healthy tissues, healthy organs, healthy body systems and therefore a healthy body. It is also important for healthy blood flow to eliminate the toxins and metabolic waste in the body! Remember, you're only as healthy as how well you eliminate. That's true for our thoughts, our body and our cells!

Getting the right oxygen and nutrients to the cells, and removing toxins and waste, can only be accomplished by ensuring healthy blood flow within the circulatory system. While most people are aware of the primary vessels in our body such as veins and arteries, they are not aware of the magnitude of micro vessels within the body. Our micro vessels are so small that you could fit 10-20 or so of them into the diameter of a single human hair. These micro vessels account for approximately 74% of our circulatory system. The experts tell us we are electric beings first, chemical second. It means that without the proper production of ATP, our bodies would not be able to spark the electrical and chemical reactions required to make our heartbeat or our brain think.

Furthermore, science has proven at any given moment the body is emanating and radiating energy. The Law of Attraction underscores the importance of energy as it states we attract "like energy". In considering this, it is clear why it is essential to nurture our bodies. Without our health, our bodies will cease to produce the energy required to manifest our desired thoughts. Without the mind's ability to think at its highest capacity, we won't have the mental acuity to envision and manifest all the things we want in life.

Moving into a metaphysical realm, the reason we must have a healthy body and a positive attitude is because everything in the physical world and the universe can be felt through the body. This is done through vibrating energy. Everything in this world is made up of energy. It is everything we see and feel as well as the way in which we vibrate, interact, and communicate with one another. Interpreting this energy is precisely how the body "feels" and communicates with other people—or rather other bodies of energy. In order to truly "know" someone, you don't interpret their words, you interpret their energy first.

Going deeper into the connection between how the body interacts with the mind. The subconscious (or emotional mind) is where we store feelings as structured energy—the cells of recognition that correlate to our emotions. Remember, thoughts create feelings, which are felt and executed through the physical body. I cannot stress enough the importance of keeping the body healthy in order to carry out the mission of the mind, which are the things you want to happen in your life.

Thoughts are the language of the brain. Feelings are the language of the body. How we think and feel creates our state of being. In understanding this concept, you can see how every thought or idea causes a physical reaction in the body. On the flip side, you can see the body is the conductor of energy and deliverer of information back to the brain to analyze and ponder as thoughts and emotions. In short, our bodies are simply the mind's connection to the physical world. To put that into perspective, think about a recent trip you took. The actual transportation occurred in a car or train or a plane. However, the trip itself was the experience, not the vehicle in which you traveled. In the same way, our bodies are simply the containers, or vehicles, that provide the physical experience.

The Brain Is the Connector

Most people confuse the mind with the brain. The brain is an electronic switching station that alters the vibration of the body. The brain has codes or "cells of recognition" (structured energy) that contain memories of the experiences we've had in our lives.

These structured energies are created by two sets of tools: The five senses and the six mental faculties of the mind. They can also be changed or deactivated using the same tools, either by your own thoughts or other external forces. Using these two sets of tools you can deactivate existing cells of recognition associated with your past and replace them with new structured energy that aligns with the success you desire. This is the basic principal behind recoding and resetting your mindsets.

When you learn something new, and start to think in new ways, you are causing your brain to fire sequences, and patterns in different ways. In doing so, you begin to think differently, which results in new choices. New choices lead to new behaviors, which ultimately produce new experiences with new feelings and emotions. This, in turn, influences how you think, which is when the (thinking) mind becomes the (feeling) body and the (feeling) body becomes the (thinking) mind.

How you put this into action is through repetition of certain concentrated thoughts on any given subject. Remember, thinking a thought based on feelings and emotions resides in the subconscious mind, which cannot differentiate between what is real and what is imagined. If repeated enough, the subconscious mind has the power to convince itself to believe it and trigger thoughts into action which causes a physical change in the brain's nerves and muscles. As a result, this brings the change you are seeking.

The brain is at least 75 percent water and is made up of approximately 100 billion nerve cells called neurons. These neurons make new connections by exchanging electrical and chemical information with each other. The more repetition among the neurons' activities, the stronger the connections. The stronger the connections, the stronger the signal to activate the genes that control your hormones. By thought alone, you can immediately activate the production of hormones by changing your thoughts. It really is *"mind over matter!"*

From this process of building new cells of recognition, you will see life in a new light and direction. It is at this point you will realize there is no limit to what you can do!

The brain is the switching station that alters the body and the mind to become one.

You must become aware of the fact that you are not your name. You are not your body. You are not your mind. You are the one who uses the body and the mind to carry out your purpose by thinking, reasoning, and planning. You are your soul.

The soul is the essence of your true self which guides you through the journey and mystery of life, much like your own private guidance system.

The more you study and understand this life power within you, the more you can connect and become one with it. When you begin to think, act, and be the person designed by your soul, rather than your brain, you will discover your Divine hidden powers.

The "spirit" is whole and complete Divine power. The soul is the *offspring of the spirit*, yet infinitely part of the whole, much like the cup of water from the ocean. It's holographic in nature and is continuously trying to regain its oneness with the spirit.

Our conscious awareness of our oneness with the Spirit is the greatest secret to success and happiness. Once your mind and heart are open to this powerful awareness, you are never the same. With this understanding comes a Divine sense of peace; you never think badly of yourself because of your awareness of who you are. You are a Divine power. You are love and happiness. You simply ARE marvelous Divine power.

The Universal Mind

The universal mind is ALL forms of energy in existence. Energy is everywhere and everything that we see, touch, taste, smell, and hear. Energy is the empty space or "ether". It is what everything in the universe is made of, and everything we can access.

The universal mind is a form of energy (ether, static, and potential energy). It moves and travels at the absolute maximum and highest rate of vibration. It is universal power. When we align ourselves with our souls, we become one with the universe—or rather we vibrate at similar energy levels. According to the Law of Attraction, like energy attracts like energy. It is in this space where we can draw upon the static potential energy of the universe to transform itself into the mental images and thoughts we hold in our minds. Once this energy is "captured" within our thoughts, it can be transformed into reality in the shape of dynamic and physical energy.

Through aligning with our true self and concentrated thoughts, we have the power to influence and convert static potential energy into dynamic energy by the power of consciousness of thinking thoughts. This is how we create and manifest in our life.

However, there is a difference between thoughts and *"active thoughts."* It is not enough to occasionally "think nice thoughts," you must actively focus your concentrated thoughts to create your desires. Thoughts are creative substances that shape our realities and have a direct impact on our lives and the lives of others, even though we cannot see, touch, taste, hear, or smell thoughts. Just like static universal energy, a thought will not transform into dynamic energy on its own until it has been instructed through our minds and bodies to do so. Our job is to shape, direct, and activate our thoughts into creating the desires we want.

An active thought can then be repeated over and over, which is a process called concentrated thinking. When you practice concentrated thinking, you influence static potential energy from the universe and convert it into dynamic energy in a physical plane.

CHAPTER SIX
The Paradigm

*"There is a thinking stuff from which all things are made,
and which, in its original state, permeates, penetrates and fills
the interspaces of the universe. A thought in this substance
produces the thing that is imaged by the thought."*
~Wallace D. Wattles

What is a paradigm? Can we change it? Who is responsible for it? Can we control it? Where did it come from? When and how was it formed? By who? Why aren't we aware of its power? Why didn't anyone teach us about it? All these questions are valid, and we need answers in order to understand the significant impact of the paradigm in our lives. You can think positively all you want, but if your paradigm is weak or "not aligned" with what you want to happen in your life, you will feel stuck and blocked from fully achieving what you desire.

Paradigms are your core beliefs shaping the pillars of your reality. They are the habits and learned behaviors which become your governing systems of how you live your life. Through the Prosperity System, you can learn to recode, rebuild and remake yourself by first altering and shifting your paradigm.

Our paradigms are not always as conscious as we would like to think. Sometimes we accept the idea of how powerful they are but, deep down, we don't really believe or understand them. Our acceptance of them is purely an intellectual process which takes place within the thinking conscious mind. Acceptance, however, is not the path to change. Change occurs when we align with our new paradigm, which resides in our subconscious. It is only then when we can successfully apply the mind-power techniques for real transformation.

It's time to reconnect with your Divine hidden power. With this power, you will shift and change your paradigm at will and by choice. When you do this, you control your paradigm and your life.

Your paradigm is the mental posture you create for yourself and how you choose to live your life. In short, the story of your mind (your mindset) becomes the story of your life! Paradigms determine the actions you DO and DO NOT take in life based on your past experiences, learned behaviors, and external influences such as your parents, friends, and even the media. Your paradigm is the master key to either your castle or your jail cell.

Beliefs are the building block of your reality. They vibrate within you every day, 24 hours a day, seven days a week. They are structured energy (cells of recognition in your brain) that affect everything you think and do. The structure of your paradigm most likely has empowering beliefs that resonate at a high energy level, and even more likely, limiting beliefs that weigh you down and block you from succeeding. You can often hear your paradigm whispering things such as *"you can't do it"* or *"you're not smart or good enough"* or *"you don't have enough money."*

Paradigms control everything about your life. They create the beliefs you have about your health, finances, sexuality, relationship, family, logic, effectiveness, productivity, perception, abilities, and so on. No matter what area of life you are evaluating, you have some sort of engrained idea or system of what to expect, or a perceived outcome that relates to that area of your life.

Beliefs are just as necessary to the mind as organs are to the body. Just like you must have a heart, lungs, liver, brain, and other organs for your body to function properly, the mind can't function without beliefs to guide your thoughts. Beliefs give you a construct in which to find meaning behind (and understanding of) what is happening in your life.

How Aware Are You?

Fish swim in the water all the time, but do they understand they are swimming in a substance called water? They do not know their existence depends on water, and that it connects them to a whole world of other bodies of water. They know this is where they live and it is their world, but they have no awareness of what their world truly is, nor the opportunity that surrounds them. It is the same with birds; they know they fly in the air, but they do not know what air is.

As humans, we live according to our paradigm (structured energy, cells of recognition) but we are unaware of its power to create our lives. This paradigm controls every aspect of our life, yet most of us haven't even heard of it! Some know it exists, and even fewer understand they can change it. Those who do possess this awareness and understanding often do not know *"HOW"* to change it.

For you to control your paradigm, you must understand everything about it, including how the mind works as well as the system itself. This process of understanding is crucial to your success because awareness and understanding precedes action and transformation. To begin this process ask yourself these questions:

1. What do you desire in life?
2. How long have you wanted this desire?
3. Why haven't you already achieved your desire?

65

These are valid questions and deserve an answer in order to move forward in life.

It is highly likely the only thing stopping you from achieving what you want are your limiting beliefs followed by inaction or the correct action.

Remember it is not what you believe IN that brings results, it is the belief in YOURSELF and the power of your mind that brings results. It is the **belief in the "belief"** itself. It is important to believe you have the power within you to create anything you want if you choose to do so. That's the key!

Now, let's dig deeper into the mind. One important question you must ask yourself is this: *When was the paradigm formed and by whom?*

Remember God created the world and the three stages of human life. In stage one, you were a child and your paradigms started to develop outside of your control. In many cases, your parents, and others who were close to you, instilled their own beliefs and perceptions around every aspect of your life such as how to make money, your health, your relationships, productivity, business and about everything that matters to you.

You can also ask yourself some questions... were there a lot of arguments in your home when you were a child? What kind of language was used around the house? How do you think those variables impacted the energy levels in the house? Were they positive, supportive, and fun? Or were they negative, limiting, and dark? How do you think they impacted your own belief system as an adult?

Guess what? This is exactly what is controlling you today. Your belief system began to develop from birth and was most likely formed by the words and actions of others when you were a child. At such a young age, you had no choice—or concept—of how you wanted to shape your paradigm. The trouble is, once your paradigm is formed, it's difficult to change, but certainly not impossible!

Become aware of all these questions to gain insights into your current paradigm and find answers that help you know what needs to be addressed.

We have the power to choose, and the power to change. The good news is because your paradigm is formed by thoughts, feelings, and actions, it can be deactivated, changed, and erased by the same tools using your will and imagination. God gifted us the power of choice and the power to change.

PARADIGMS ARE FORMED EARLY

IDEAS BECOME FIXED

Diagram 8
The Infant Mind

As you can see in Diagram 8, prior to the development of our conscious mind as infants, our reasoning faculty was almost in an "OFF" position. It is only as we grow in age and awareness it begins to turn "ON." As parents, it is important to be aware of what you say and do around your children—particularly as they are developing their own reasoning faculty and conscious awareness. As young children, whatever is said and done around them will leave an impression on their subconscious mind. This will construct habits and beliefs and lay the foundation for their future behaviors and actions.

Another way to think about how your paradigm was formed is to imagine that, as a baby, your subconscious mind decided to have a huge party where everyone was invited; good, bad, kind, cruel, generous, greedy, successful, lazy, loving, honest, and deceptive, etc. It's really a mixed bag of characters. When all your guests attended your party, they each left their footprints, impressions, fears, doubts, worries, anxieties, perceptions, habits, and feelings on you. They dumped it all in, consciously or unconsciously. Neither you nor they knew any better. Everyone was just living their life according to what they knew—good, bad and everything in between. *Why?* Because at that age, you were like a sponge. Your subconscious mind was wide open for anyone to imprint anything into it without questions or permission and that became reality for you.

However, as you entered the second stage of life, adulthood, you started to develop your reasoning faculty, which is your ability to accept and reject information and actions. Now, when your subconscious mind decides to host a party, you hire a bouncer at the door who acts as a bodyguard between the entrance of your conscious and subconscious mind to protect you (reasoning faculty to accept or reject) from the people or ideas you don't want to let in. Suddenly, you become aware of the impact these people are making on you and how they are affecting your life.

The problem is when you first hosted the open-door party as a baby, you already let everyone, and their beliefs, in the door. Now that you have become aware of what these "guests" have been doing to your paradigm without your permission, it's time to get rid of the unwanted guests. Those guests are the ones that are negative or critical to your desire to change. They are limiting your beliefs, blocking the pathways of high energy toward prosperity.

It's time to dive into the subconscious mind to finally clean up the remnants of past parties. You will keep who and what you want to stay and trash the rest. You must delete, deactivate, and eliminate them from your mind in order to take control of your life. You must recode, reset, and reboot your mind. It will take work, but in the end you'll be able to create the life YOU want and not the life others have defined for you.

CHAPTER SEVEN
The Tools & Laws of the Mind

We are the only creatures on this planet that are given two sets of tools: The five senses (sight, hearing, touch, taste, smell) <u>and</u> the six mental faculties, which are:

1. **Imagination**
2. **Reason**
3. **Will**
4. **Memory**
5. **Perception**
6. **Intuition**

You become a creator when you are aware of the powers found within each of these six mental faculties and start consciously using them. Utilizing these powers of the mind will transform your mindset from a competitor mindset to a creator mindset. There is a huge difference in living life as a creator—that's when the fun begins! These tools are mainly to design, create, change and control your paradigm. Here are the tools and how to use them.

Imagination
Your imagination is what makes it possible to envision your future. Without it, you lack direction. In essence, you don't know where you are going. Imagination is the key to designing your life. It is a powerful and critical tool allowing you to create pictures and images of the things you want in the privacy of

your mind. As Einstein said, *"Imagination is more important than knowledge."*

In this mental faculty, you can explore infinite ideas and opportunities and turn them into detailed images of how they might come to be in the physical world. In other words, you are discovering the static potential energy surrounding you, and you begin the process of willing it to transform into dynamic energy.

Arnold Schwarzenegger, a successful actor, politician, and body builder reaffirms this concept in the following excerpt from the book, *"Creating Visualization for Beginners"* by Richard Webster:

> *"When I was very young, I visualized myself being and having what it was I wanted. Mentally, I never had any doubts about it. The mind is really so incredible. Before I won my first Mr. Universe title, I walked around the tournament like I owned it. The title was already mine. I had won it so many times in my mind that there was no doubt I would win it. Then when I moved on to the movies, the same thing. I visualized myself being a famous actor and earning big money. I could feel and taste success. I just knew it would all happen."*

Similarly, let's look at what champion golfer Jack Nicklaus wrote in his book *"Golf My Way"*:

> *"I never hit a shot, even in practice, without having a very sharp, in-focus picture of it in my head. It's like a color movie. First, I 'see' the ball where I want it to finish, nice and white and sitting up high on the bright-green grass. Then the scene quickly changes, and I 'see' the ball going there: its path, trajectory, and shape, even its landing. Then there's sort of a fade-out, and the next scene shows me making the kind of swing that will turn the previous images into reality. Only at the end of this*

71

short, private, Hollywood spectacular do I select a club
and step up to the ball."

One of the most powerful functions of the subconscious mind is its lack of differentiation between what is real and what is imagined. Whatever you program your subconscious mind to do through your imagination, you will transform it into whatever you desire.

Reasoning Faculty

Your reasoning faculty is the ability to accept or reject anything. This tool is perhaps one of the most powerful, simply because it is the faculty that gives you the power of choice. Remember, because you have the power to choose, you have the power to change.

You can use this tool to fine tune and adjust your paradigm by choosing which ideas and beliefs you want to keep or discard. It is entirely up to you. No one can take advantage of you unless you allow it, nor can anything pass into your consciousness without your permission.

Will

Your will is the driving force and motivation behind everything you do. It is laden with discipline. This tool gives you the ability to maintain focus despite any distractions that may come your way. If applied to your power to choose, your "willpower" to change is magnified. The more you focus and concentrate on achieving change, the stronger your ability to manifest it will be.

Memory

Memory is the storage house where your experiences are available for your conscious mind to use, search, and pull information relevant to a situation. Resonance energy plays a big part in memory. All memories and experiences have correlating cells of recognition, or structured energy. When you think of a certain memory, it will play out exactly how you remember it in your mind. You will "feel" the feelings associated with that memory. Those feelings are powerful!

Memory creates a structured energy of pictures, voices, and feelings associated with it, which becomes imprinted as cells of recognition. A memory itself will remain unchanged. However, through the five senses and six mental faculties of the mind, you have the ability to change your perception toward it—particularly if it is a memory that influences your decisions or beliefs.

Intuition

Your intuition is the tool that enables you to sense feelings and energies from another living being or situation. Intuition is knowing something before you think it and it often comes in the form of hunches, tips, gut feelings, or that small voice inside your head.

Intuition is knowing something without knowing how you know it. It is your ability to observe a situation without the interference of reason or perception. It is also known as the sixth sense. It is the language God uses to communicate with you. It is important to acknowledge it with gratitude and trust.

Perception

Your perception is the process in which you analyze a situation based on your existing paradigm. It is like your own personal lens of how you view and interpret the world. Perception becomes your reality regardless of its truth!

For example, if we ask ten people to think of a dog, most will see and feel different things about dogs according to their own experiences. Some will love dogs, and some will fear them. To give you an example of just how differently perceptions can range, I'd like to share a short story with you:

There was a man who was getting ready to move to a new town. He packed his belongings and started driving, and just as he was only a few miles away from entering the new city, he stopped at a general store for gas and something to eat.

Outside the store he noticed an old man sitting on a rocking chair and decided to strike up a conversation with him. He asked the man "What kind of people live in this town?"

The old man replied, "How were the people from where you came from?"

The traveling man said, "Oh, they were mean, gossiped a lot, and were not friendly. They would steal you blind. They couldn't be trusted."

The old man looked at him with a blank stare and said, "You will find that people here are the same as where you came from."

Then the traveling man left.

A few hours later, another traveling man from the same town was also moving into this new town. He happened to stop at the same general store to get gas and snacks. He also noticed the old man on the rocking chair and started a conversation.

"I'm moving to this town. Can you tell me what kind of people live here? Again, the old man said, "How were the people where you came from?"

The traveling man said, "Oh, I am going to miss them a lot. They were so nice, generous, loving, and they cared about each other."

The old man looked at him. He smiled and said, "You will find that the people here are the same as the ones where you came from."

The moral of this story is your belief system influences how you view the world around you. It is your perception of the situation that dictates how you view life based on your paradigm. This is your reality regardless of where you go. You cannot leave it behind, nor can you escape it. It lives in you and the only way to change it is to alter your paradigm.

The Laws of the Mind

The laws of the mind are so simple, yet so misunderstood. The laws are exact and work the same for everyone. Everything in the universe is subject to laws. We know there are laws of gravity, physics, electricity, sounds, and everything in the cosmos.

If you want to create the things you desire in life, you must play by and obey the laws of creation and manifestation by becoming aware of the laws of the mind and know how they affect and impact your life.

Here are the laws and principles of the human mind:

1. **Thoughts Are Real Cosmic Waves and Forces**
   "A man is but the product of his thoughts. What he thinks, he becomes." ~Gandhi

   There is no doubt thinking is the real business of life. The pure fact we have the ability to think makes us unique. All creation begins with thoughts—the instrument that directs our consciousness and shifts paradigms.

   Thoughts are creative substances that influence static potential energy shaping our reality. Even though we can't see, taste, smell, or touch our thoughts, we can't deny their existence. We can, however, activate them at any given moment.

In fact, we think between *50,000-60,000 thoughts per day*. That's a crazy number! Even more astounding is 90 percent of those thoughts are the *same thoughts!* When we continuously think the same thoughts, we continuously make the same choices, which of course, result in the same behaviors and experiences. This predictable behavior imprisons us in a vicious cycle of thinking and experiencing the same thing repeatedly. Though many people fight to break the cycle, the chains run deep from their paradigm and they often give up and start to believe that they could not change.

That's how powerful our thoughts are. They are real forces that affect our life.

2. **The Mind is a Conductor and Emitter of Thought**
We are constantly sending and receiving thought energy from different sources—specifically from other people—consciously or subconsciously. Also, we are affected by outside sources such as radio, TV, internet, and other media channels. We send and receive thoughts according to our own energetic vibrations. The beautiful thing about exchanging energy is you can help change another's low energetic vibration into a higher frequency by sending energies of love and healing. However, in the same way, others can send and receive energies of low vibration too. So you must be mindful of what energies you are sending.

What's key to vibrating at a high energy level is to think good thoughts about yourself and others. When you do this, according to the Law of Attraction, you will attract other high vibrating energies that will bring more positive situations and experiences into your life.

3. Law of Attraction

All thoughts are comprised of energy, which gives them the ability to magnetize and attract similar resonating energies. This law explains the creative process through which the inner world (unseen) gives birth to the outside world (seen) and manifests the circumstances and events of our lives (the physical).

The Law of Attraction does not respond to words, it responds to feelings (personal energy), and does not differentiate between what is real, imagined or an illusion. It simply responds by way of cause and effect.

The Law of Attraction is a blind law; neither good or bad, moral or immoral. It is only bound by individual demands (personal energy). It is through this law that you attract thoughts, events, circumstances, forces, and people that align with your levels of energetic vibration.

4. Law of Control

We are constantly and forever experiencing thoughts, but we can accept or reject them with the help of the tools found within our reasoning faculty. To that end, we have the power to choose. We can choose to accept negative energy and situations into our lives, or we can choose to reject them.

5. Law of Insertion

We have the power and ability to insert any thought of any type into our mind with the help of our own personal will and imagination. This is a powerful law, but hardly ever used.

The great thing about this law is the thoughts, images, and feelings don't have to be "real," they only need to be imagined.

The power behind this law occurs when we insert these thoughts, images, and feelings into our mind, such as abundance, success, power, healing, love, health, confidence, or whatever it is we desire. We bring them into our life.

6. **Law of Connection**
Most people think we live in one big world. This is wrong. We live simultaneously in two independent worlds. The inner world and the outer world, which are connected. What happens in the inner world affects the outer world and vice-versa.

The inner world is comprised of all the thoughts, feelings, beliefs, and reactions within our consciousness. We are constantly reacting in the inner world as a result of whatever is going on in the outer world.

The outer world is made up of all the circumstances, events, people, and other forces in our environment. We must realize we allow the outer world to influence our results.

Please understand we do not necessarily want to ignore the outer world. But the truth is, we must focus on the inner world to control the outer world by using the mind power techniques.

Each one of these two worlds has its own possibilities and dynamics—as well as its own laws and realities. Both the inner and the outer world feed into each other, but most people use the inner world only to react to things rather than to create what they want.

7. **Law of Cause and Effect**
"The law of cause and effect is the law of all laws." ~Ralph Waldo Emerson

Whatever you put out into the universe comes back equal and opposite. It is the action and reaction, which are equal and opposite. That's how powerful this law is in life. Every cause has its own effect, and every effect has its own cause. Nothing happens accidentally. Everything happens according to the laws.

The key here is to focus on the cause. When the cause is strong and effective, the result—or effect—will return as something strong and effective as well.

8. Law of Vibration

"If you want to find the secrets of the Universe, then think in terms of energy, frequency and vibrations." ~ Nikola Tesla

Everything in the universe vibrates in constant motion as energy. Everything is energy. Look around you. Everything you see is energy: the walls, the chairs, the bed, the TV, the book you are reading. They are all made up of energy—the difference is the rate of vibration. When we increase thought energy to a much higher frequency, we move from static energy into dynamic energy, we manifest our thoughts. This is the great secret of life!

Resonance is the exchange of energy between two things and is the phenomenon that influences a certain energetic pattern to shift and change into something else.

I truly believe this law must be well understood in order to obtain health, prosperity, and any other desires. To do this, we must vibrate and emit high levels of energy.

Science has now proven we are a mass of energetic vibrations contained by our physical bodies. This is referred to as "Bio-physical energy".

Vibration is the law and language of the Universe. We think on different frequencies, or levels of vibration. In order to make demands about the things we want in life, we must learn how to match the energy of those things. Whatever it is you want in life, be that energy and you will attract, construct, and manifest it into existence.

Part of the process of matching your energy to what you desire is to maintain a healthy lifestyle—particularly one that facilitates adequate production and regeneration of energy giving you the clarity of mind needed to make the changes in your life you wish to make.

9. **Law of Polarity**

Everything in our marvelous universe has an opposite, or more specifically, a "polar opposite" of the same thing. For example, a magnet has a positive side and a negative side, but both ends are part of the same magnet. Here are some more examples of opposites and their corresponding wholes:

- ✓ Right—Left (Direction)
- ✓ Hot—Cold (Temperature)
- ✓ Health—Disease (Health)
- ✓ Wealth—Poverty (Finance)
- ✓ Happy—Sad (Emotion)

Everything in life must have an opposite for it to make sense. Otherwise, we would not be able to fully understand or appreciate it. We cannot measure and feel the difference if there is only one side to things.

This is one of my favorite laws. When we understand the power of this law, we understand the power of consciousness and how it arranges and rearranges itself for the things we want.

The law of polarity might be compared to a river, except it flows in two directions. For example, wealth and poverty have a midpoint on the scale of consciousness. It's the tipping point of consciousness. At this juncture, the river flows in two directions, opposite from each other.

I am reminded of a Native American legend clarifying the law of polarity as it is a timeless parable from the Cherokee:

> *An old Cherokee chief is teaching his grandson about life.*
>
> *He says to the boy, "A fight is going on inside of me. It is a terrible fight and it is between two wolves. One is evil—he is angry, envious, greedy, arrogant and is full of lies, self-doubt, resentment and inferiority.*
>
> *The other one is good, and full of joy, peace, hope, love, truth, kindness, generosity and faith. This exact fight is going on inside of you and every living person on the planet earth."*
>
> *The grandson thought about it for a minute or so until he finally asked his grandfather, "Which wolf wins?"*
>
> *The old chief smiled and simply replied, "The one you feed."*

Our main objective in our path to prosperity is always to shift our consciousness into a state of what we want to exist. The tipping point between ordinary and extraordinary is set into motion when we feed our consciousness with the things we want, rather than the things we don't want.

When we feed the wolf of prosperity, we begin to have dominating thoughts of positive and powerful energy. Using some of our God-given tools, such as will and imagination, we activate a circuit of energy that powers the action and reaction process of creation (cells of recognition in our brain).

Consider the law of polarity—opposing ideas cannot both be held at the same time. You cannot be healthy while you are constantly thinking thoughts of disease. You cannot be wealthy and constantly thinking thoughts of poverty. It is possible to switch from one polarity to the other, but you cannot hold both in the mind simultaneously. You cannot stand up and sit down at the same time. You must choose one or the other.

10. Law of Gestation

Just as every seed has a gestation or incubation period, so do your ideas. Nature does not take short cuts or skip seasons. It does not provide instant results. You must plant and cultivate your desires before you can harvest them. There are no exceptions to this law. The same exact thing applies for your thoughts and ideas to manifest. Think of your ideas as spiritual seeds that once planted will grow when the time is right, they will bloom into physical results. In the same way, your goals will also manifest when the time is right.

CHAPTER EIGHT
Immersion for Understanding

"Knowledge is the observation of a fact. Knowing is the inner experience of the fact."
~Vernon Howard

Understanding comes at different levels with the use of contemplation and concentration when acquiring this knowledge and understanding of the power of your mind. You must first learn it, then assimilate, absorb, and apply it to your life. Applying the knowledge will give you a deeper understanding and conviction, which will lead to confidence and faith in your ability to manifest. When you have faith as a vibration of energy, then you are well on your way to manifesting anything you want.

What is energy? Energy is the universal life from which all thoughts, feelings, and things are formed. Each one of us is made of the same energetic force regardless of your belief or faith.

Life energy (universal mind) is the basic building block of our existence, which is made up of infinite amounts of static potential energy. Simply put, this means universal energy can manifest itself through us via our ability to think thoughts and put them into action. Our interaction with this life force energy is so significant without it we would cease to exist. When we come to fully understand this, we can begin to comprehend just how much we matter and how important our role is within the universe. As G.I. Gurdjieff, Philosopher and Author, said...

*"Everything is dependent on everything else,
everything is connected, nothing is separate.
Therefore, everything is going in the only way it can go.
If people were different everything would be different.
They are what they are, so everything is as it is."*

Energy exists in two different forms: invisible waves and visible particles. The energy is there regardless, but these are the forms in which it presents itself. All energies are connected and communicate within itself through time and space.

Since everything is connected, it means what we experience in our inner world has the power to change and affect the outer world. As we change our vibrations of energy using the tools found in the laws of the mind, we change our realities, circumstances, and life situations.

Energy Immersion

Everything is energy and vibration. Like vibrations attract and dissimilar vibrations repel. As you've already learned, energy cannot be created or destroyed. Anything that ever was or is yet to come has always been here in the form of energy since the beginning of time. With this understanding, everything you want, and desire already exists. You only have to acknowledge it and become aware of the information you have been given and implement it. The reason you don't already have what you want in life is because you have been thinking and acting in ways that don't align with the energies you are seeking.

To get what you want, you must think, feel, and act in a way that aligns with the type of energy you want to attract. Again, if you are in alignment with your true self, you can connect with the highest levels of static potential energy and bring it into existence by thinking concentrated thoughts as though your desires have *already* happened. Then, you simply let go and allow it to happen with faith, confidence, and an expectation of its fulfillment.

The consistent feeling of the vibration of energy creates an energetic field that surrounds your entire body. It is this electromagnetic field that attracts the forces, events, situations, and people you want in your life. From an internal perspective, this energy field is a product of your structured energy (cells of recognition) which emit a vibration. This vibration is what connects and attracts other like-energies to you—both positive and negative. Moreover, this is a prime example of how biology and spirituality merge into a unified field to create your path to prosperity. In short, the makeup of your energetic field is the sum representation of everything you have ever thought or experienced up until this point in time. This unique, and extremely personalized energetic field responds to both internal and external forces in mysterious and magical ways.

When emitted, this energetic field surrounding your physical body, extends and spreads great distances and connects with other like energies within the universe. The stronger your concentrated thought, the stronger the energy that resonates within your energetic field, and the faster you can influence the static energy of the universal mind. This will allow you to manifest the things you desire.

What's important to understand is you can't just "learn" about manifesting. You must align with your true self, and do the work to manifest what you want. This may take days, weeks, months, or even years before you are in a balanced state of mind that will allow you to take full control of your mind. Reading self-improvement books or going to seminars or workshops is not enough by itself. You must regularly practice the techniques found in this book. Ultimately the power lies within finding inner balance in a loving and spiritual way that will allow you to combine your mind's power with your spiritual beliefs, and the laws of the mind outlined in Chapter 7. Once you do this, you will open the floodgates of prosperity.

Imagination Immersion

There is no higher form of creation than imagination. We are visual creatures. "Picturing" what we want is one of our most powerful tools to lead us down the path of prosperity. Unfortunately, we tend to focus and visualize the problems more often than the solution. However, in practicing positive visualizations, we will not only attract like energies, we will ultimately shift our mindset and make a positive impact on our lives.

Our imagination is a Divine gift. It is the workshop housing our ability to shape and shift our realities through mental images. These mental images are the seeds which are planted in our subconscious and grows into our conscious awareness, which sprout into the actions which eventually bear the fruits of our desires.

Imagination allows us to live a more exciting, beautiful, and adventurous life and helps us break through from the logical into the visionary world.

Visualization

To successfully plant a seed that bears the fruits of your desires, you must focus on the pictures you design in your imagination.

I invite you to participate in a visualization exercise:

> Imagine what your life will look like when you have achieved the "prosperity" you desire. Remember this is your experience and the definition of prosperity may be different for you than it is for your neighbor. Create images in your mind, examine them carefully, and experience (feel) them fully.

Infuse your images with as much detail as possible using the five senses and allow yourself to get emotionally involved with what you are seeing and feeling. Let go of your old beliefs which have held you back in the past. Allow your mental picture to grow until you "feel" as though it is happening in the present—in the "NOW!"

Pay attention to your feelings and notice if there is something blocking you, such as fear, doubt, or worry. Let go of these emotions and persist with your visualization until you can experience it in a way you feel confident, energized, powerful, and happy. The more detail you can paint into your visualization, and the stronger you can experience the emotions of it, the stronger the influence of static energy providing a faster manifestation.

Remember, manifestation will not happen overnight (even though on rare occasions it can happen quickly). It usually takes time for the subconscious mind to absorb the picture and feelings to accept it as truth. You must be persistent and dedicated in practicing this exercise. When you bring your mind back into the present, don't feel disappointed if what you saw in your visualization does not already exist, nor if you're not immediately able to picture your desires in perfect details.

Don't let a blurry picture stop your progress. Keep going! Many people when they first try this exercise can only hold a faint, blurry image in their minds. Do not worry, the image will get clearer with practice and it doesn't have to be perfect to make a difference. Just by practicing this simple exercise you have rearranged the energy patterns within your body as well as the ones surrounding you. You are one step closer to prosperity than you were a moment ago.

Feeling and Fueling Your Thoughts Through Emotion

When you envisioned your future, what emotions surfaced? What did you feel? The key is to *"feel"* rather than simply think, wish, or hope the things you want will become reality someday in the future. When you see and imagine ideas, those images exist and have life. You want to embody them with strong feelings and emotions as if they already exist. It's one thing to think thoughts, but it's much more powerful to *"feel"* how it will be when it's your reality. When you can visualize and feel the emotions in the NOW moment, you can let go and trust the universe do its magic to bring those things into your life!

To feel is simply a physiological reaction to stimuli, such as a thought. With repetition, these reactions become structured energy cells within your brain. You can call this process "planting the seed" or "designing the blueprint" of your desires. Ultimately your feelings are the way in which you connect and draw upon the powers of the universal mind through the help of the subconscious mind.

With enough repetition of a feeling, the brain activates a chemical reaction in the body that releases corresponding hormones. Those hormones—both positive and negative— influence our epigenetics, or how our cells "read" our genes and result with an emotion. Over time, any repetition of the same emotion will inevitably create a mood or a state of mind.

This is why emotions are so important in manifesting prosperity. Our emotions are a product of our thoughts, but it is our emotions that are the power source fueling our thoughts and driving us forward into action and into life. Emotions also have a higher impact on our energetic field and magnetizes our dominating thoughts and feelings—both positive and negative.

Perspective: Are You the Star or an Extra?

Let's go back to our visualization exercise now that you understand why it's so important to feel and become emotionally involved in your visualizations.

Think back to what you saw in your visualization, were you experiencing it or were you watching yourself from an outside perspective? Most people visualize the things they want but don't *see or feel themselves* in the picture. That's why most people are extras in their own movie. They see images, but they do not include themselves as part of the experience.

Creating images or pictures of the things you want to accomplish is like creating a movie in our own mind. It becomes the story of your life which is composed of hundreds of mini stories involving other people.

Just as an actor embodies the energy and mindset of the character they have been assigned to play, you too must embody the energy of the new person you want to become. In order to successfully become that person, you must have the knowledge and awareness of what's involved in the process of building and becoming that character. The more you develop your level of awareness to its highest peak possible —in order to recognize the flow and exchange of energetic forces that surround you — the more you can influence the events and people that show up in your life to help you become that character; the "new you."

I believe we can learn anything by doing it either physically or mentally. Initially, most people have a hard time effectively visualizing enough detail in their images to include what they really want—and that's okay. With practice it will become clearer and more real. The clearer the visualization, the more powerful it will be in attracting and influencing the static energy which surrounds us.

My team and I conduct powerful seminars and workshops on the Entrepreneurship and Leadership Mindset. Part of the teaching involves the art of visualization. I sincerely hope you get the chance to attend one of our seminars in the future whether on land or at sea. It will reinforce everything you are learning in the book and will take you to a new level of understanding and life.

Subconscious Mind Immersion

Whatever you impress on the subconscious mind will be expressed as conditions, experiences, and events in your life. The subconscious mind is the "principle" you must understand and work with for real manifestation to occur.

What do I mean by working with a principle? Think about electricity. The basic principle of electricity is simply the flow of electric current running along a conductor. To use electricity, we don't change the principle, we work with it to create things that benefit us, such as TVs, stoves, cell phones, etc.

It is the same with the subconscious mind. We must work with it to create things that benefit us. We cannot work against it, because in doing so, we are working against our true selves. And that causes us to be out of balance. This will create a lower energetic level of vibration.

Also remember your subconscious cannot differentiate between what is real, and what is imagined. Moreover, it will respond to anything you feed it without judgement—much like a mirror. A mirror will show you an exact reflection of how you look in its reflection. It does not judge, change, or question you; it simply responds to whatever it sees. In this case for example, your physical image is a representation of your current reality; to change it you must access the power of the universal subconscious mind—the life force energy—to formulate an idea, such as changing your physical body shape (putting the idea into action to alter your reality). The mirror now shows a reflection of your new reality, which is a new body. This is how the subconscious mind works. Reality follows consciousness. Supply follows demand. In this example, you can see how you have the power to change and influence your reality by feeding your subconscious images and feelings of how you want to live your life.

The key to manifestation is to open the door between the conscious and the subconscious mind. Guarding this door is the analytical or critical mind. This door can be thick or thin, which determines how difficult it will be to break through. Typically, the stronger your paradigm, the thicker the door. The thickness of your door determines how difficult it will be for you to accept the seeds you are planting in your subconscious.

In a nutshell, the thicker the door or "barrier" between the conscious and the subconscious, the more difficult it will be to reprogram your paradigm. But it can still be done with enough practice!

Spirit Immersion
"Thinking is the soul talking to itself." ~Plato

We have learned the importance of the mind-body connection, but we have not yet discussed the third part, the spirit. In connecting with the spirit, we elevate our consciousness to a whole new level. Our spirit is the voice inside our head that seems to whisper hidden knowledge. When we become aware of this Divine power, we can transform from living a mediocre life to an extraordinary life.

Your spirit is your soul, your true higher self. When you connect with your spirit, you are connected to the Universe. You begin to see you are within everything, and everything is within you. When you live in alignment with your spirit, you are content with just being in the NOW, with full confidence, trust, and expectation that the universe will guide you down the path toward fulfilling your highest potential.

When you live a spirit-led life, a huge burden is lifted from your shoulders because you now understand your true value and you learn the only opinion that matters is your own when it comes to defining the life you desire. The door between your subconscious and conscious mind is completely open and the limiting beliefs that once consumed your paradigm are eliminated. You are fearless, powerful and limitless.

You can connect with your spirit at any time. Though you cannot "see" it, it is always there, and it never leaves you. Connecting with your spirit is much like tuning into a station on the radio. Spirit is always communicating with you; we just have to learn how to tune into its frequency. Sometimes, our spirit's messages are intense, communicating with our consciousness in the form of intuition, or "gut feelings."

You can experience your spirit in the NOW. You will hear it in sounds that surround you when your analytical mind quiets, or you will feel it in your bones. Your spirit exists in the stillness of thought, and the quietness of the NOW.

You can often recognize people who are living a spirit-led life as those who serve others and shift their focus from themselves to thoughts of others. They also often live with an abundant mentality because they know who they are, and they are fearless. They know "fear" is nothing more than an illusion and the universe will always guide them down the right path.

To live in alignment with your spirit is to see opportunities rather than problems. You are aware how thought energy works and know it is entirely in your control as to whether you allow this energy to influence you in a positive or negative way.

Individuals who are connected to their spirit are always learning. They allow everything and everyone to be their teacher or coach and are open-minded to accepting knowledge from others. To be in alignment with your spirit is to be self-less. Those who give and are grateful for what they have been given, activate their spirit, which in turn, gives back many times — and they truly prosper.

Intuition Immersion

When Einstein was asked about his secret of success, he said, *"It is the result of intuition; an inner knowing."*

You also have this power of inner knowing. Your intuition is the tool that enables you to pick up feelings and energies from other life forms and communicate an inner knowledge before you even think it. It is pure wisdom exuding from your spirit.

It is also called an instinct, or "hunch". It's the small voice in your head, your sixth sense, or gut feeling. It is when you know something without knowing how you know it; your ability to observe a situation without the interference of reason or perception. Intuition is the channel the subconscious and the universe use to communicate with you.

When you become aware of this powerful universal wisdom of "intuition" as a tool you already have, it can be used to open your mind and heart to prosperity.

When you are looking for meaning and guidance for the things you want in life, the answers will not be the voice of God shouting at you. It will come with a small inner voice, a feeling, an instinct, or your intuition. When you live by your intuition (instinct), your life will be enhanced—especially when you align and balance your intellect (logic) and instinct. Then the results will be even more powerful.

93

We were all born with this intuitive power. It is a spiritual gift designed to protect us and sustain life in a practical way. It is our intuition that guides us in such a way that is both mysterious and magical. We are not the only creatures to possess intuition. This is clear when you see birds migrate south for the winter. The animal kingdom relies on intuition, which is automatic in nature.

As humans, we are genetically hardwired with this mechanism. We don't have to be taught how to use it, we only need to be aware of it and learn how to be in tune with it. The challenge we face as we mature is that we have been taught to rely solely on our five senses and intellect for evidence, and not to rely on our intuition. We have been conditioned to place too much trust in technology, rather than to listen to this powerful tool already available to us.

We all have internal senses that extend beyond our physical five senses. Those senses send us messages on a daily basis to alert us to danger, seize an opportunity, or to get an insight. They are our inner compass and personal GPS system. If we allow it, our instincts can become the bridge connecting us from where we are now to where we are going.

Consciousness Immersion

Consciousness is an awareness which is paying attention. When you pay attention to the energy of the universe, you are connecting your consciousness to the highest levels of frequency and information.

Consciousness is the ability to recognize what you are thinking, as well as how it is impacting your reality. It is awareness at the highest level.

Scientists have documented human consciousness which influences life force energy, or the essence of everything that exists. But it is not a well-known or accepted concept in society. As such, many people disregard and reject the idea. The fact is, your consciousness and life force energy are constantly interacting with one another through your energetic field (sometimes called an "aura"). It is this interaction which allows you to transform the life force energy or static potential energy into dynamic energy or material form.

I am not here to claim we know all there is to know about the universe and life. But, we often don't know enough to shift our consciousness to support us in all areas of our lives. This knowledge and awareness is what we will use to begin the process of mindset-reset.

Let me explain it this way:
- ✓ We want more money but are always concentrating on the limitations and the lack of it.
- ✓ We want a new and better job, but we constantly say there are no new jobs.
- ✓ We want good health but are always thinking thoughts of illness and disease.
- ✓ We want a new relationship, yet we tell ourselves there isn't anyone out there.

You get the point. Our reality follows our consciousness. Supply will follow demand. The key here is to shift the tipping point of your consciousness to cause a mindset shift towards what you want to accomplish in life (not what you want to avoid).

Abundance is a vibration of energy—a feeling. Feelings trigger emotions, which bring about an action, which emits a corresponding energetic vibration. Remember, what you emit attracts other like energies, whether it is happiness, sadness, apathy, excitement, etc.

Whatever you want in life, you must feed your consciousness with those thoughts. Your consciousness is like a garden. It will produce what is planted. If you want tomatoes, you plant tomato seeds. If you want apples, you plant apple seeds.

We don't doubt the nature of the harvest. We don't plant carrot seeds and expect to get cabbage instead. It is the same thing with seeding our thoughts and ideas into our consciousness. If we want health, abundance and success, we must plant thoughts of health, abundance and success.

Willpower Immersion

The will is a very specific and powerful energy. It is perhaps the single most powerful force we have. Our will is simply this: No matter what the situation is, we *ALWAYS* have a choice. No one can take this power from us. Our willpower is also our ability to hold and focus our mind on a single idea or thought without any distraction within the NOW moment.

While our ability to choose is inherent, our ability to maintain focus is learned. The best way to enhance your focus is to find what captures your full attention. Some call it your passion, others call it your purpose or your heart's desires. Whatever it is, what gets your attention will be the easiest to focus on. Learning to maintain focus takes willpower, but the process in doing so is much like meditation—it takes practice, but once you master it, it becomes second nature. Focused thoughts are also concentrated thoughts. We have already learned the power of concentrated thought. However, when combined with willpower, we can direct them into becoming new cells of recognition (structured energy) in the brain. In a sense, our willpower through concentrated thoughts makes our brains accept an idea.

We activate this tool by making decisions and, most importantly, acting on those decisions with persistence, courage, and determination to get the things we want in life. This willpower is essential and a prerequisite for creation. We can develop it by imprinting and the seeding techniques. The more we use our will, the more energy it gains and the more momentum it builds.

The best way to enhance willpower is to become interested in the object of your desire. The greater the interest, the greater attention you should give it. The greater attention, the greater the interest becomes, and so on. As you have learned, energy goes where attention goes. So, interest and attention can be cultivated by contemplation and practice to enhance willpower.

CHAPTER NINE
The Power of Sex Energy

Wait, what? Sex energy? *Yes, sex energy.* You might be wondering what sex energy has to do with mind power and manifesting. Understanding sex energy is part of discovering your secret hidden powers, and it is one of the best ways to create the life you want when you understand it.

Napoleon Hill wrote a whole chapter on sex energy in *"Think and Grow Rich."* I value and respect the book so much and read the chapter on sex energy many times in order to grasp and understand what it meant! I have read other books and researched the subject from a variety of sources on the power of sex energy, in order to gain more clarity on this energy and how to use it.

Unfortunately, even among those who understand sex energy and what it means in terms of manifesting, very few people talk about it. We tend to stay ignorant about our sex energy and the power it provides us to manifest the life we want.

It's interesting that the greatest teachers, shamans, top achievers in business, inventors, artists, and most politicians have thunderous personalities because they understand what sex energy means. They are often some of the wildest, most adventurous, interesting, and fascinating characters— whether they are consciously aware of their high sex energy or not.

What it boils down to is this...Our ability to focus and concentrate our thoughts and emotions on a single outcome — along with the help of our will and imagination when we are in the present "*NOW*" moment —allows us to create whatever we desire in life.

Sex energy is powerful creative energy!

When we are in the *NOW* moment and able to fully engage in an idea without any distractions, we let go of time and space. Then, as the observer, we remove our energy from the familiar, known life and environment and invest our energy and awareness into the unknown field of all possibilities that exists for us. That's how our consciousness becomes part of the universal pure consciousness. They merge and we become pure consciousness. This is the sweetest spot in this state of being. We can plant whatever seed we want in life for its manifestation.

If you want to experience this inner power in your life, whether to create new opportunities, heal your body, or create new relationships, you must become aware of the power of the *NOW* moments in your life. Most people are unaware of what these moments mean in terms of creation. In NOW moments, the past and future no longer exist. Your full focus is in the present moment. When you experience this state of mind, you have captured the power of sex energy. In this moment, you are existing in the sweet spot of turning possibilities into reality.

Once you enter the NOW moment, you become aware of the vast field of empty space containing nothing but frequencies of potential static energy and information of every possible creation. In these NOW moments, there is no judgement; you are no longer thinking or analyzing ANYTHING, nor are you activating any structured energies that exist in your

subconscious mind. You are nothing but pure consciousness. In this state you are aware of how you can merge your structured energy (consciousness) with the pure energy of the universe. In this powerful convergence of consciousness, you can create whatever you desire in life.

Using the power of sex energy is just another mind-power technique you have to create the life you desire. It is a very powerful tool, once you understand and know how to apply it.

Just as there are many ways and options to paint a picture or make spaghetti sauce or travel from point A to point B, using sex energy is just another way of creating and manifesting. The difference with sex energy is that you add more powerful fuel to the fire.

What is Sex Energy?

Sexual energy is life energy—it's our birthright.

Sex energy is one of the most powerful forces of energy we have as humans. When we are driven by it, it can ignite courage, imagination, persistence, and creativity. But, if we are ignorant about it, we associate the use of it only from the physical aspect. Sex energy includes the act of sex itself, but there is a lot more to it than just that.

Sex energy is the energy we emanate from our bodies to the universe. It is natural, incredibly powerful, and readily accessible. I believe anyone who chooses to use the knowledge of the power of their sexual energy can be rewarded in a very meaningful way. You can use sex energy to reap a variety of benefits. It's a key to health, happiness and wealth. But if you feel uncomfortable with it because of certain beliefs and culture, at least choose to learn about it. But, don't worry about working with it if it doesn't feel right for you.

It is important to become knowledgeable about it and aware of the different uses of channeling this energy. Sex energy has

many benefits including living a longer life, having a healthier body, and the ability to be an extraordinary achiever.

The goal of ordinary sex is either for pure pleasure or to conceive a child —and there is nothing wrong with that. But why not use it for other purposes to create other things?

As Jeffrey Tye explains in his book, *Sex Magic*:

> *"The most powerful moment of human existence is the orgasm. Sex magic is the art of utilizing sexual orgasm to create a reality and/or expand consciousness. All senses and psychic powers are heightened during orgasm. It is a moment when a window opens to the unlimited abundance of the unlimited universe."*

During sexual engagement, we are completely in the present NOW moment. No one is worried about the bills, problems at work, the neighbors, weather, politics, school, screaming kids, in-laws, phone ringing, or even the fierceness of a fire truck siren. The only thing that consumes our mind is experiencing each detail of each NOW moment beyond the five senses. This focus resonates high vibrations of energy reconnecting and uniting us with our oneness with the universe.

During sexual encounters, we reconnect for a short period of time with the cosmic life force energy. In the process, we get a unique glimpse of our oneness and Divine nature of who we truly are. When we understand the power of sex energy and how it can be channeled, as well as have the awareness of how to use the power of "being in the NOW moment," we are given the opportunity to imprint (visualize) and seed (feeling as something has already happened) what we desire in our life. That is power—multiplied power. Sex energy is a way to mobilize our creative power of being in the "worry-free state" to generate the result we desire in our life.

In short, this process can be described in three steps:

1. **Our mind creates a clear intention**. We are specific about what we want. We can clearly visualize it and express it through thoughts which make up the electrical charges we send out into the universe.

2. **Our body provides the fuel.** When we are in the moment of creation, we have a way to imprint what we want. Feeling the emotions ahead of the experience creates a magnetic charge, and when that charge merges with the electrical charge of our bodies, it creates an electromagnetic field that surrounds us. This field of structured energy is a beacon that emits and attracts like energies of the universe.

3. **Our spirit guides the result.** Through our electromagnetic fields, we emit our true intentions into the universe. Once they have been projected, a match of energies is made within the life force energies of the universe. The attracted energy is then catapulted back into our electromagnetic field, where we can transform it from static potential energy into physical reality. These energies can come to us in the form of forces, events, opportunities, people, or other experiences needed to make our dreams a reality.

Let me share an example with you of channeling sex energy...

Let's say you are on a vacation, taking a cruise from Miami to the Virgin Islands. While you are on the cruise, you decide to go on the upper deck to watch the sunset. You are dressed up, looking and feeling good.

The weather is beautiful; there's a gentle breeze and you can hear the waves of the ocean and see the sunlight shimmer on the brilliant, aqua-colored ocean. You even spot dolphins swimming alongside the ship.

As you look around, you suddenly notice a beautiful lady, (or handsome man as the case may be) standing 30 feet or so on the other side of the deck watching the sunset as well. She really gets your attention.

She is your type — not only does she have perfect hair, but you also like her choice of clothes and the colors she is wearing. You get excited about the way she is dressed. What's more, she has a confident posture which gets your wheels turning. You are interested in her. You are in the NOW moment. You are focused solely on her.

You make up your mind up you are going to approach her and start a conversation with her. Your brain is now in high gear, operating at a higher frequency of creativity. You are imagining things with this person, and your mind is working on how you are going to approach her. You are asking yourself unconsciously, what should I do? What should I say? How should I act?

You want to win her attention and heart. You are emotionally involved with this idea of talking to her and are fully focused on this task. You are 100% engaged in the NOW moment and have nothing else on your mind. You are present. You have made up your mind you are going to get the job done regardless of what happens. You are going to approach her and persuade her through easy conversation to ask her out.

You approach her with courage, confidence, focus, determination, and a certain expectation—you are on a mission! On a subconscious level, your energy is already flowing directly into her heart and she is feeling your intensity and courage, your persistence, enthusiasm, and confidence because you are vibrating and radiating energy toward her. That's why she is feeling it as well.

As you introduce yourself and start a conversation, it isn't long before you have a date!

Now, let's analyze what happened so you can understand how this powerful sex energy —including all the focused thoughts of intensity, courage, persistence, enthusiasm, determination, imagination, and willpower — helped you achieve your desire. You want to store this combination of "sex energy juice" in a bottle to be saved for future use, so you may drink from it when you need a boost.

Ask yourself how did this encounter begin? How did she show up there to watch the sunset with you at the same exact time you were there?

The answer is simple: *You were the cause! She was the cause! You were both in resonance and attracted to one another. This is the Law of Attraction in action!*

The important factor in embracing sex energy, is to embrace the single focus of your goal, eliminating everything else from your conscious thoughts. You are truly in the "NOW" moment when you tap into your sex energy.

Make Sex Energy Work for You
Practice being grateful and thankful for your awareness and understanding of the power of sex energy. Have a positive

belief of its power and the many benefits it brings to you in all aspects of your life.

Most people don't understand the power of sex energy and often deny its power to create. As H. Jackson Brown, Jr., the author of *A Father's Book of Wisdom* said, *"The greatest ignorance is to reject something you know nothing about."*

Being open-minded and willing to learn, discover, and understand the power of sex energy is one of the *"special keys"* to accomplishing what you want in life. When you learn to shift your manifesting ability into a higher gear using your sex energy to create your desires and ideas, you become supercharged with tremendous force — unlike anything you have ever experienced before. It will enable you to "create" and "cause" your thoughts and goals to manifest into the physical world.

When you use your sex energy to create, either consciously or unconsciously, it's like driving a Ferrari in 6th gear. This experience is so exhilarating it catapults you into the NOW moment, which is the moment when your mind is in a state where it is ready for imprinting and seeding into the subconscious. That's the key! The ultimate secret of creation is being in the NOW moment and using the Law of Insertion to infuse and inject what you want to happen in your life during this very powerful NOW moment.

Sex Energy Channeling

Our objective with channeling sex energy is first to understand, digest and practice it over and over. Channeling sex energy is an art and skill like anything else. It is not enough just to know about it. You must experience it. It requires certain skills and techniques: *willpower, discipline, focus, patience, and the art of visualization.*

In sex energy channeling, you are using your mind and body's energy powers. With the help of your will and imagination directed toward a goal, you can hold the images and the energy of the thing you want to happen in your life in the NOW moment in a worry-free state. You can achieve the "already happened" feeling, which is the key to manifestation! *Do you see and feel how powerful this is?*

The key to sex energy channeling is simply and easily explained by switching off the mind and body from thoughts of physical action to thoughts of some other nature: *business, projects, inventions, health, healing, and so on.* Our expanded consciousness during this intense NOW moment allows us to transfer this intensified rate of vibration toward the things we want to manifest—and that's what gets the job done. We embody the thing we desire, we feel it strongly, and we eliminate everything else from our focus.

Being in the NOW moment can be accomplished in many ways; sex energy is one example. Of course, there are other options, such as meditation, being out in nature, listening to music, or whatever it is that gets you into a NOW state of being.

Using Sex Energy to Become Extraordinary
When you discover how to increase vibrations of thoughts, you become extraordinary. The vibrations get to the point where you can communicate with sources of knowledge, wisdom, and insights not available at the ordinary rate of vibrations. You are thinking and acting in a certain energetic way.

In essence, you are building new cells of recognition in your brain which can be called upon to create. Therefore you need to have "creating" sessions. Think of it as though you are using your thoughts and emotions as a tool, much like a hammer and a chisel, to carve your reality from the raw material of the universe. When you *become* that energy, you are on your way to manifest the things you desire. When you master this skill, you can become extraordinary with mindfulness awareness.

Sex energy, or being in the NOW moment, can lead to the birth of a baby, as we are all aware. But sex energy can also give birth to things in the physical world such as goals and visions of the things you want. It helps to bring these goals into reality quicker.

How do we stimulate our minds and raise our energy to higher rates of energetic vibrations to serve our intense desires and turn on our creative imagination and willpower? I believe the desire for sex on the physical level is at the top of the list of stimulants. Of course, this requires the body's energy to be fully functioning and healthy. When the body is functioning optimally, we have a greater sense of "well-being" and can tap into this energy more readily.

We can stimulate our minds when we blend sex, love, and romance to enhance our sex energy and take it to a higher level. It will create confidence, courage, peace of mind, and persistence.

Being healthy and having healthy blood flow throughout your body and brain allows you to fully tap into the natural energy of your body and mind.

When you are in a state of the worry-free NOW moment, it is the perfect state of mind to use the mind-power techniques to create your vision of the life you desire. It is in this heightened state of being that your subconscious is wide open for higher connectivity with life force energy, and where the lines of communication between mind, body, and spirit are at their peak. This powerful moment is reached just before or during an orgasm. Again, it can also be achieved through creating these feelings of your own making or recalling this moment from your structured energy in stored memory.

When you are engaged in lovemaking, make yourself consciously aware of the feelings and sensations you are experiencing in this blissful moment which is void of distractions and worry. Imprint this energy in your consciousness so you can use it to create new cells of recognition at will.

This sexual energy of being in the NOW moment helps us to dissolve ordinary limitations, blocks, and other obstacles in life. It is during this moment we feel euphoric and free. What's more, it gives us a glimpse of our true, infinite potential and power. At any given time, you can choose to recall this energy to feel this way, as needed.

When you are at your peak of highest vibrations and in the NOW moment, you are as close as possible to the cosmic energy vibration of the universal mind—which not only contains intelligence, but also substance. Again, this is why sex energy is so powerful. When you are that close to ether vibration, then you can almost reach out and physically grab (manifest) anything you want.

The key is to match the energies of your imagination and concentrated thoughts and release them out into the universe during this magical moment. When this energy is released, the Law of Attraction begins as if you put forth a magnet to attract like energies of static potential energy. Then you can absorb them and set things into motion. Again, sex energy is the highest level of vibration during which your subconscious mind is wide open to receive new ideas and possibilities.

Making Sexual Energy Effective

When sex energy is at its peak, we boost tremendous and powerful electrical charges in the NOW moment of creation. It will zap your thoughts, ideas, images, and desires with a zillion volts of power to imprint what you want in life into the subconscious mind in a very powerful, magical, and mysterious way. It influences and converts the static energy in the universal mind into dynamic energy in our physical world. It does this by our concentrated consciousness of thought energy.

By now you know healthy ATP (Adenosine Triphosphate) energy is needed to be in vital and optimum health, not only to enjoy the physical act of sex, but also to focus your mind on achieving your desires while riding the wave of sexual energy. It is not easy, but it can be done. It needs practice, practice and more practice in order for it to become easier.

One of the best ways to accomplish this is by using visuals of your desired goals, whether it's to acquire money, get a new job, buy a house—or whatever it is you desire. It is a lot easier to look at an image just before, during, or in the moment of being in the NOW moment (orgasm) than trying to utter or verbalize an affirmation or even a feeling, especially at the beginning stages of using our sex energy power.

Visuals convey clear intentions of what we want to accomplish. Remember, we think in pictures and we can only imprint effectively when we match the vibrations of what we desire during the NOW moment. The subconscious only understands the language of NOW and cannot differentiate between what is imagined and what is real in terms of pictures or feelings.

The big question we must ask ourselves is *how is it possible to communicate with this source of knowledge to expand our consciousness?*

We are partners and one with cosmic life force energy. We are all connected and share in this power of the oneness of mankind. We are energy vessels bathed in this vast cosmic life force energy and are intricately plugged into it. We are constantly extracting from its energy. Without it, we would cease to exist.

When you become aware and understand this powerful sex energy and use it consciously, then your connection to it expands in very powerful ways and you can draw even more energy from it. It's as if you change your batteries (energy) and it becomes much easier to create what you want in life, as well as communicate with your higher intelligence for guidance, insights, ideas, wisdom, or whatever information you need.

Deeper Understanding of Sexual Energy

Being in the NOW moment is crucial; the universal mind is an everlasting NOW moment, so when you are in this state, you are connected to the universal mind. Again, it is when you are in this state you can most successfully imprint what you want.

Sex energy is focused energy and is the opposite of being distracted with scattered thoughts. You need to have a focused mind in order to be fully present in the NOW.

Be aware that you are creating the thoughts and emotions you are experiencing during or at the moment of orgasm. Whether you know it or not and whether you like it or not, you are creating something.

From this moment on, pay close attention to your thoughts and emotions when you are in the NOW moment and learn to consciously create the life you want and NOT have default creations.

Words have tremendous generative power in them. When you verbalize what you are creating and actualizing during the "feel good" moment of sexual energy you enhance the electrical charge. Be very specific with your intentions during the peak of your sexual energy, regardless of the way it takes to get you there.

Using Sex Energy in Selling

We are always selling or buying ideas when we communicate with each other. Whether we are selling for business, or selling ideas to our spouses or children, we are constantly persuading or being persuaded to do or buy into something on a daily basis. We are either buyers or sellers and are constantly switching roles. *But, how do we successfully buy and sell?*

110

People can be influenced by appealing to their emotions. That's where sex energy comes in. For example, when approaching customers, successful salespeople have this energy constantly in their state of mind, whether they have it consciously or subconsciously. Wouldn't you agree that they approach buyers with the same intensity, willpower, and excitement of pursuit as did the person on the cruise ship in our earlier example? This demonstrates that you don't need to be actively engaging in sex to call upon its energy to approach others with ideas and services with the same enthusiasm and determination. All you need to do is recreate the heightened experience of concentrated and focused thoughts of being in the NOW moment to use it for other pursuits.

Channeling Sex Exergy

When you drink from your bottle of sex energy (stored NOW moment experiences) and combine it with persistence, determination and discipline, you are successfully channeling your sex energy. You are on a mission and you become unstoppable. Once you have mastered the art of channeling your sex energy, you can use it to instantaneously make an impression through a handshake, your tone of voice, your overall presence. It is this radiation of sex energy that fills us with personal magnetism and charisma. It can be an immense power for good. The people you interact with can immediately sense this energy and are more likely to respond to you in a favorable way. This magnetic current will promote peace and harmony to the person practicing it, and to the people who are feeling the energy.

Sex energy is a blend of focus, courage, determination, and being in a "worry-free" state of mind. This state of mind destroys fear of the past, present, and future and allows your Divine light to shine in your life. The clouds and barriers will disappear, and you will find the source of your secret, hidden powers and finally free yourself from the blocks which stopped you from reaching your goals before.

111

Sex energy has always been and will always be with you. It will awaken you to your true infinite potential of how you can enhance your life and reconnect to where you came from in a Divine way.

This is very powerful knowledge and insight very few people know about or have even heard about. You are now one of the lucky and enlightened people. Congratulations!

Remember, it is your birthright. Use it to manifest your dreams. Have *FUN* with it! It is yours to enjoy.

CHAPTER TEN
What Do You Really Want to Happen in Your Life?

"No more effort is required in order to aim high in life to demand abundance and prosperity than is required to accept misery and poverty." - Napoleon Hill

I work with people from all over the world who come from all walks of life and cultures and ages. During our sessions, my mission is always to train and bring awareness to everyone's purpose, vision, and goals, and teach them how to accomplish them. The biggest issue I see most often is that people do not have a clear understanding of what they "really" want or what their real purpose in life is.

It's sad to go through life without an inner awareness of your connection to your purpose. It's like a light bulb without a lamp. This kind of disconnect leaves you unfulfilled regardless of what you have accomplished. It is up to you to discover you purpose or the things you were created to do with the people you were meant to affect. It is important to understand the power you generate from aligning with your purpose.

"The purpose of life for man is growth, just as the purpose of life for trees and plants is growth. Trees and plants grow automatically and along fixed lines; man can grow as he will. Trees and plants can only develop certain possibilities and characteristics; man can develop any power which is or has been shown by any person

anywhere. Nothing that is possible in spirit is impossible in flesh and blood. Nothing." ~ Wallace D. Wattles

Our purpose explains what we are doing with our life and addresses the "why" of our journey. For example, when we travel anywhere, *why* are we travelling in this direction? What's the purpose?

Our vision explains how we are living our purpose. Our vision is the promise of what we will one day become. *Who am I?* It is the total picture of who we intend to become. *What's the vision?*

Our goals enable us to realize our vision. They are the smaller, digestible activities which break down our vision. They are the milestones of achieving what we want in life. Our goals define the direction and speed at which we travel. *Where are we going first? How long will it take to get there? Where are we after we achieve them?*

As you can see, goals give our life direction. In order to achieve them, they must excite, empower, reward, and challenge us.

There are primarily two reasons why people don't achieve their life goals:

1. **Non-Specific Goals**
   Most people don't have any *specific* goals. Everybody has *desires* and *wishes*, for example, to be healthy, wise, have a lot of friends or have a lot of money, etc. The problem is these goals are not specific. Goals must be very detailed, written down and reviewed daily. **If you don't have a clear vision of where you are going, you will never get where you want to go!** Your goals must be specific for your subconscious mind to be able to manifest your desires. For example, if your goal is to "move west," create a vision for how far west. What country? What city? What street? What type of home? If

114

you are general, you won't hit your mark. Be specific when you create your goals.

2. **Weak and Small Goals**

   Of those who have goals, their goals are often *too small*. They do not motivate or make a profound difference in their life. If that's the case, it is possible they are simply not in line with their true purpose, and they feel a sense of disharmony; their goals are not energetically charged.

   The task is to reevaluate the goals and discover what it is you truly want. Reconsider who you really are. It is then you can revisit your goals to turn them into "big-picture" goals which will ignite your willpower and imagination and cause you to take actionable steps towards them.

If you don't already have what you want in life and are struggling, it's because you have not yet convinced your subconscious mind to accept the thoughts and ideas you want. It means you have been adopting, accepting, and holding a vibrational energy pattern that does not match with your desires. Your goals and desires must be more powerful than your paradigm!

Discovering Your Purpose

There is a divine plan and purpose for each one of us. We came to this planet with a divine plan which was uniquely designed for us, but it is up to us to discover it.

In general, our primary purpose in life is to *serve humanity*. The question that remains is *at what capacity*?

Personally, I have been guided to discover my Divine purpose to help and show people how to activate their secret, hidden power and how to open their minds and hearts to prosperity. If you recall, I had several events and "aha moments" of clarity when my intuition spoke and flashed through my subconscious mind with messages and an awareness informing me I had a special talent to help people learn how to become prosperous and find their purpose in life.

When we discover our purpose and design our vision, we have created our mission. It becomes the light that guides us through our journey. Here are some steps to help you find your purpose:

1. Ask yourself what is your purpose in the Divine plan? Then, quiet your thoughts and listen as your intuition speaks to you.

   Your purpose is embedded in your passion of the things you *love* to do. You will also find hints of your purpose embedded in what you absolutely, passionately *hate* to do as well! The awareness of both aspects will help you discover your purpose and connection to your higher self.

2. Ask yourself what would you really like to do if money was no object? What interests you? What excites you? What is it you would enjoy doing even if you didn't get paid for it? Or, what is it you absolutely dislike doing?

   Knowing what you love and what you hate can ignite your intuition to discover your passion, as well as boost your probability for success.

3. When you ask yourself those questions, focus on what images you see, the emotions you feel, and the words you say. What comes to mind? Write them down! You will have many ideas and things coming to you. With some added structure, those ideas will become your goals.

4. See your goals in your mind's eye. Feel them. Hear the voices affirming how you've done it. Then, start with the one that excites you the most. What do you value about this goal? The words that come to you are your values. For example, these can be things such as adventure, excitement, helping others, respect, influence, charities, fame, power, or whatever comes to mind.

5. Write them down and ask yourself which of those values are most important to you? The answer will be your foundation and core values of why you are doing it. This is your "BIG" why. This will be your purpose, the direction you should take for your life!

Get Creative with Your Talents

Use your answers as a starting point to create the images of who you want to become and start seeing yourself with these values. Add the details to your vision, become a master at using the five senses, and make it as real as it can be. It does not have to be in high definition to start with—you will get there. Add colors, audio and feelings to make it energizing and exciting.

Be creative! Don't let your current reality limit your thinking! You have the tools and understand the laws of the mind. You know how to ask questions if you get stuck. Ask the right questions and you will get the right answers. Remember, the quality of your life is dependent on the quality of your questions.

As you are designing the images and the feeling of what you want, ask yourself what proof must you have in your vision to confirm you have achieved your goals? What demonstrates you have already met your goals and achieved what you wanted? Then, take a moment and listen to your inner self. Allow your spirit to flow and add to your images. This could be based on the impact to you, your family, spouse, parents, business, church, community, country or the world.

Rewarding Yourself is The Fuel

There is always a motivation as to why we do certain things. It is the way we have been wired. There is always a payoff. We must convince ourselves there is a reward. We don't necessarily want a million dollars, but we want what a million dollars can do for us. In truth, we are not in pursuit of a physical object, we are in pursuit of how it will make us _feel_!

When we go to work, we do certain things that are worth something. If there is no reward and no pay off, why would we want to do anything? However, when we convince ourselves there is a reward in the form of money, success, recognition or incentive, we do the work necessary to achieve it!

CHAPTER ELEVEN
Mind Power Techniques

*Mind-power techniques are the tools to **seed, imprint, and affirm** into your subconscious in order to open the flood gates of prosperity into your life.*

Seeding

Seeding is planting in your consciousness what you want to manifest in the form of a vibration of a specific energy. It is a feeling. You seed by vibrating with the feeling (energy) as if you *already have* what you want.

When you get emotionally involved with the things you want, you embody the attributes of a magnet. You become magnetized with a specific vibration of energy. To do this you have to become aware that there are two primary emotions in life... love and fear. In other words, we do things based on gaining pleasure or avoiding pain. Either we love what we want or fear what we do not want.

When you are seeding, you are matching the vibration of the things you want by creating the patterned cells of recognition in your brain. Then you communicate the pattern to the life force energy to get a response back in the form of events, circumstances, forces, people, and more.

When you are vibrating with the feelings of worry and doubt, you are seeding worry and doubt. When you vibrate with confidence and abundance, you are seeding confidence and abundance. In comparing the vibrations of worry, doubt, fear, confidence, joy, happiness, and abundance, it's important to notice that they are completely different in vibration and feel completely different from each other. You have to "feel" the emotion of what you want, rather than the "gripping" emotion of fear of what you don't want!

Effective seeding means operating from the perspective of already having accomplished your desires rather than the idea that you will eventually have it some time in the future. To seed, you must combine your intention of what you want with heightened and turbocharged emotions. This pairing is what conditions your subconscious mind to accept and *believe* what you want is already here. It is an "*already happened*" feeling.

This conditioning will feed your mind of thoughts, reinforcing the feeling. Your thinking will strengthen your feelings, and so on. In short, you must seed daily. Ideally twice daily; once in the morning and just before you go to sleep. Then allow the universe to do its magic!

Visualization

Visualization is imprinting your consciousness with what you want to create in your life. When you create the mental images of the desired outcome in your inner world, you are stimulating the mechanism that eventually makes it become real in your outer world.

Going back to our example of electricity, by itself it is useless and could be very dangerous if applied the wrong way. But when we find devices that harmoniously utilize the power of electricity, it provides multiple benefits and luxuries such as giving us light, heat, cold air, refrigeration, music, TV and more! In the same way, the static energy of the universe by itself is useless, but when we can harness this specific energy and transform it into a new reality, it can provide us everything we desire.

The mechanism you are using during visualization is creating the mental images, and most importantly, the *feelings* and *emotions* associated with your desires. This is the process of manifestation in action!

Visualizing is a sequence of mental images which are infused with as many details as the five senses can accumulate. In addition, you must add the emotions and feelings you will have when you achieve your goals.

Keep in mind, it's not just a picture, it's everything associated with that picture. Visualization is using our imagination to see something *happening to you* in the future.

This mind-power technique has been used by high achievers throughout time all over the world. It takes conscious discipline, and practice, followed by actionable steps. The more you practice it, the clearer your mental picture will become and the faster it will come into being.

If you realize that there are some similarities between visualizations and seeding, you would be correct. Visualization and seeding are closely related. When you go through the process of visualizing your future and make it feel as if it is happening NOW, you are infusing those mental images with feelings, which is how you plant the seed that will germinate to become your reality. Seeding is the process that operates on the vibrations of feelings. Keep in mind, for successful visualizations and seeding, you must be relaxed and calm (or in the NOW moment). Before you begin, take several deep breaths to slow your thoughts down and relax your body and mind into the stillness of the NOW.

The mind responds best to images and feelings, which is exactly why I so often refer to the importance of these mind-power techniques. If you practice with enough repetition, images and feelings get embedded, imprinted, and ingrained in your brain as structured energy (cells of recognition). Over time your actions coincide with this structured energy and they will begin to reprogram your paradigm. At that point, the subconscious moves you even closer toward those images, which connect you with the universe in such a magical and unexplainable way. When you experience this power, you will understand why this is the greatest secret of prosperity.

Affirmations

Affirmations are the words supporting and enforcing what you want to happen in life. They are the spoken words or the "songs" of your life. I love what Florence Scovil Shinn said, *"Any man who does not know the power of the word, is behind the times."*

When you utter words, they affect the outer world. Your spoken words and phrases have their own vibrational energy force which influences the static potential energy to convert it into dynamic physical energy. This is a powerful tool to bring your goals into your reality!

Affirmations are the easiest and simplest technique to influence the conscious mind and alter the subconscious mind to create great results. A lot of people use them for passing exams, meeting people, closing deals, and much more.

Affirmations are short and simple statements. You repeat them to yourself aloud or silently—whatever feels good and comfortable to you at the time. You can do them at home, in the shower, on the beach, in the car, in church, in the supermarket, at work — or anywhere really!

They are short statements which represent what you want to happen in your life. You should say them repeatedly. Essentially, you are feeding your mind phrases and sentences stating the things you want. You are not trying to convince God to give you what you want. All you are doing is opening your mind and heart to receive what you want by convincing your subconscious mind—the connecting link of communication—

to accept what you want as truth. Then the subconscious mind will open the channels through people, events, and other forces to give you what you want.

When you do affirmations, you are suggesting to your mind to think thoughts of your affirmations. The words and "thinking" their meaning create images, which are infused with feelings. Once you are emotionally involved, you will think more of the same thoughts. Multiple thoughts powered by emotion will spur the body into action. This is a perfect example of the mind-body connection as well as the Law of Cause and Effect.

When you first start affirmations, your mind may fight you about the accuracy of the statements. For example, when you say, "I am wealthy," your conscious mind (the critical and analytical mind) may say to you, *No, you are not!* This is a very natural response from the conscious mind.

This critical mind is part of the conscious awareness which thinks, observes, judges, compares, questions, accepts, or rejects things. It relies on past experiences to the degree of how analytical your mind is. So, the greater your analytical mind (the more you will analyze things), the less effective your power of suggestion to your subconscious mind will be. On the flip side, the less of an analytical mind you have, the more effective your power of suggestion to your subconscious mind will be.

Don't let your analytical mind discourage you. Keep practicing these mind-power techniques with diligence. Repetition is what opens the door to the subconscious mind for it to accept what you want, in order to make things happen. Do not expect to be successful immediately as the mind will certainly put up a solid fight. It is in your persistence in practicing affirmations where you will find victory. As you continue to repeat your affirmations, the analytical mind will begin to falter and say *you are not going to give up, are you?* It is at this point where you will begin to really see progress, get more emotionally involved and things will begin to tip in your favor.

When you begin new affirmations, your analytical mind moves from doubt to confidence. It is as if it is saying *"Can I be, do, or have the things I want?* ⇨ *Maybe I can* ⇨ *I think I can* ⇨ *I know I can* ⇨ *I AM who I want to be."*

That persistence and confidence creates the feeling and the energy you must have to create your desired life. This is called *"mindset-reset."* It doesn't happen overnight or with the click of a button. It takes action, persistence, determination, and perseverance. That's why you must stick with it!

As you can see, the purpose of affirmations is to create the structured energy (cells of recognition) in the brain of what you want. That's where the structured energy is stored to be used during the process of manifestation. When you are choosing your words to assemble your affirmations, be aware to use positive words to support the belief you are creating. Focus on what you want and NOT on what you do not want.

For example, if you want money, don't say, "I don't want to be poor". If you want health, don't say, "I don't want to be sick". If you go on repeating statements like that, you will become poor and sick. The reason behind this is the mind filters out the words "NOT," "DON'T," "NEVER" of your affirmation and only processes the energies of the words. It's just like if I tell you to NOT think of your car, or DON'T think of a pink elephant, what are you thinking of now? Your car and a pink elephant. This is precisely how your mind processes negative affirmations.

Affirmations and manifestation take time to be effective. It's as if you are driving your car on a narrow street and want to turn around and go the opposite way. You will have to make several turns and adjustments as you move forward—and backward! In this case, backward movement is sometimes necessary for you to move forward.

The same thing goes for subconscious imprinting using the affirmations which take you from *can I ⇨ maybe I can ⇨ I think I can ⇨ I know I can ⇨ I AM.* It is a process. You will experience a series of forward and backward movements as you reprogram your cells of recognition.

Affirmations create their own energy and they will begin to fuel themselves.

Affirmation is a process of learning. You can learn anything in life! You learned how to walk when you were a baby, how to balance yourself when riding a bike, and maybe even how to speak different languages. You learned the multiplication tables when you were in school by repeating and writing them so many times you could automatically remember them when you were tested.

The repetitions and suggestions in affirmations is the key. Being persistent in doing these mind-power techniques is the key to deliberately *tipping* the edge of consciousness into what you want in life.

The Eyedropper Effect

The eyedropper effect is a demonstration of how you can create change over time with consistent actions. Imagine you have an aquarium filled with water. Your intention is to change the clear water into red water by dropping one drop of red dye into the aquarium using an eyedropper each day.

The first day you drop the red dye into the aquarium, you see no effect. The red dye quickly dissipates. However, you continue to add a drop every day for a while. Still, you don't notice anything happen. Determined, you continue to do the daily drops, but again, nothing happens. Despite the discouraging results, you press on and continue to drop in a single drop of red dye every day for an extended period of time. Then, one day you start to see the water turn from clear to pale pink. At this point, the process seems to speed up and you begin to watch the water turn to a rosier color and then finally to a brilliant red.

That is exactly how it is with seeding, visualization and affirmations. It is the process of getting to the *tipping point* of your consciousness to create what you want in life. The eyedropper is the daily mental gym and the dye is the creating sessions you practice daily which can range from 10 to 20 minutes each day.

It took time, but eventually the clear water finally turned red and is unrecognizable from where it started. The change was not just a result of the last few drops, but rather the accumulation of ALL the times you used the eyedropper. That is how you manifest as well.

Unfortunately, most people will give up on the process and quit. They will never give the process a chance to work. Manifestation takes time, dedication and perseverance! And, it's worth it.

How to Become
We must *BE* before we can *DO*, and we can only *DO* what we *ARE*, and what we *ARE* depends entirely upon what we *THINK*.

To be a participant as a creator, not just an extra in your own movie, you must practice deliberate and intentional thinking. Only then can you begin to play a significant role in your life.

It starts with the power of words, pictures and ideas you use and allow into your consciousness. The story of your mind (IDEA) is the story of your life. In this story, you use words to speak, read, write, and hear. You also use them to generate pictures and evoke feelings (ENERGY).

The main objective of preparing the mind is to be in the NOW moment, which can be challenging at times. I like the Chinese

126

saying, *"The mind is like a drunken monkey always jumping from tree to tree."* Our thoughts can run wild and at a million miles a minute with no rhyme or reason. Quieting your mind in itself is an art and skill, and you do not have to master it right away to begin your path to prosperity. However, I will provide you with a few guidelines to help you in the process:

1. Find a quiet place where you can be comfortable and relaxed. Consciously affirm to yourself, *I feel calm and relaxed*. Repeat this affirmation for two to three minutes. You will begin to feel calmer and more relaxed.

2. Tune into your breath. Breathe deeply and slowly, and feel your breath enter and leave your body. Breathe deeply into your abdomen (*not* shallowly into your chest). Count slowly to four when you inhale, pause holding your breath, and slowly count to four when you exhale and pause before you take your next breath. Do this for 5 – 10 breaths to quiet and relax your mind and body to be ready to take the next step.

3. Consciously talk to your body and tell it to relax. With each breath, move the focus of your mind from your head to your neck, then your shoulders, arms, hands, abdomen, hips, thighs, calves, ankles, feet, and toes. Notice if you have tension anywhere in your body. Make a conscious effort to release that tension. You want to feel calm and relaxed throughout your body.

4. Once you are totally relaxed and both your breathing and thoughts have slowed, pay attention to your surroundings—inside and out. You can choose to listen to your heartbeat or feel the weight of your body against the chair (or ground if you're lying down). Listen to the sounds you hear, or whatever captures your attention. Once you find it, don't judge it, just experience it in whatever capacity you experience it.

127

Deep, slow breaths will help you relax and calm your nervous system. Remember to take deep breaths throughout your day whenever you feel stressed or are finding yourself in a negative thought pattern.

Slow deep breaths help to slow down your thoughts and make you calmer, more rested and relaxed. It's good to tune into your breath anytime you feel anxious or start to have negative chatter in your mind! Just pause, tune into your breath, take slow deep breaths, and replace the negative chatter with the positive affirmation of what you want to attract.

Gratitude is governed by the law of attraction. Remember, for every action, there is an equal and opposite reaction. When you give thanks, it triggers a reaction of receiving more of what you are thankful for in life. The more you give thanks, the more you receive — and the more effortless life becomes.

When you are grateful, you are sending out vibrations of appreciation. You are saying, *send more of the same please.*

What's even more powerful is being grateful and thankful in advance of the things you don't even have yet. That's the power of manifestation!

Gratitude is an attitude that will connect you with the main source of supply to provide even more abundance of what you are grateful for. Gratitude is a feeling; a vibration of energy. You can be grateful and thankful in every area of your life, such as your health, finances, relationships, food, people, and everything you have in your life. The more gratitude you give, the more you get of the same in return.

Being thankful and grateful is the bridge connecting you from where you are to where you are going with the things you want in life. The stronger the vibration of gratitude, the stronger and faster your manifestation will be.

CHAPTER TWELVE
Navigating the System

You and I, and the other seven billion people on this earth look exactly like diagram 7 below. The "K" stands for "knowledge" and the "I" stands for "ignorance." They are located on opposite sides of each other on the scale of consciousness.

The "tipping point" of consciousness "IS" will be found in the center. The line with the "+" and "−" represents our consciousness governed by the law of polarity (or the law of opposites), which we have already discussed in Chapter X.

Diagram 7

When we make decisions in life, we make them based on two factors: **knowledge or ignorance**. Keep in mind knowing about something and not doing (or using it) is the same as being ignorant. Avoid being ignorant by implementing what you know and take action toward experiencing it.

Follow me to the left side of the diagram. If you do things based on ignorance—and do them long enough—you start noticing you're not getting the results you want, nor do you feel good about yourself, which triggers self-doubt, worry, and fear.

On a vibrational level, these feelings resonate at low energetic levels and put you in a state of anxiety, which suppresses your desires and motivation. It can also lead to depression, disease, and disintegration. In this state of being, you are disconnected from source and power. Saint Clair Lewis was right when he said, *"We don't die, we kill ourselves."*

Now let's move to the right side of the diagram. If you do things based on knowledge, you understand what you are doing and experiencing it. This understanding gives you good, calm feelings and a sense of confidence in what you are doing.

Confidence resonates at a high energetic level and, as the law of attraction confirms, it will attract more energies of the same vibration, such as faith. Our bodies too will feel this energy in the form of improved health and wellbeing. Operating based on knowledge allows you to express yourself, which accelerates your path to prosperity as creation becomes easier. On the right side of the diagram, you are connected to source and power, where our *CREATOR* intended for us to be.

To be in control and navigate this system, you can start by periodically observing yourself. If you are feeling good, excited, happy, stop to consider what kinds of thoughts you are having. What is it about them that makes you feel this way? What do they entail? Each time you experience an emotion, stop to observe your thoughts and contemplate your feelings and what they mean to you. This by itself is another exercise to help you understand who you really are. Analyzing your thoughts will help you go from where you are to where you want go. As it relates back to diagram 7, you can begin to move from the left side to the right.

This system will give you an immediate measurable confidence of who you are and your ability to create your life. This is the secret of your personal power.

CHAPTER THIRTEEN
The Four Stages for Transformation

"You can't change anything by fighting or resisting it. You change something by making it obsolete through superior methods." - Buckminster Fuller

To create successfully, you need absolute focus and concentration, which takes immense willpower to avoid distractions and becoming disappointed. When you go into your imagination to train your mind to design the things you want, you are training your consciousness to vibrate and match the energies of your desires. For these energies to match, your conscious mind must be in sync with your paradigm (or belief system) of the subconscious mind.

It becomes obvious. If you want health, confidence, abundance, and prosperity, you must think parallel thoughts. Those thoughts will not come into existence if they do not vibrate at the same level of health, confidence, abundance, and prosperity. To match the energies, you must *believe* in them with all your power. Thinking of them and believing them are two different things. When you believe in them, you bring emotion to the thought and imprint it on your subconscious mind. By utilizing the mind-power techniques found in this book, along with your will and using your imagination daily, you will succeed!

Prepare to Prosper: Service above self

Knowing what you want in terms of goals and understanding and how the laws and tools of the mind work is not enough. You must add *spiritual power* into your mind and heart to have lasting prosperity.

Spiritual power comes in the form of serving others. You may be wondering how you can serve others. You can serve in any way that feels right to you, whether it is donating money or time, contributing to a cause, or simply doing random selfless acts of kindness. All that is required to serve is the will to do good without any expectations or something in return. When you serve, you automatically elevate your positive vibrations, which sets the stage for attracting prosperity.

Prepare to Prosper: Detox Your Mind

Everything you have learned up to this point has prepared you to prosper, but there is one very important step you must take...you must detox and cleanse your mind.

This step is a *"MUST DO" step*. A mental detox clears away all the blockages keeping certain energies from flowing to and from your mind and heart. As it is with any detox, you must rid your mind of all the junk to make room for new structured energies to fill your mind. First, start by getting rid of everything you don't want in both your inner and outer worlds:

1. **Outer World:** Detoxing your outer world could be a physical act of giving things away or cleaning out your car, home, garage, or office. Whatever you need to do to feel lighter, energized, and ready to start living your new life. By clearing unwanted or unnecessary items from your surroundings, you are creating a vacuum or "emptiness" in your outer world. As your subconscious mind reinforces what you want, it will begin to work its magic of manifesting what you want.

2. **Inner World:** The inner world is a little more complex as it must be cleansed of unwanted thoughts, bad energy and emotions blocking the way to open your mind and heart to prosperity. To cleanse your inner world, you must release all of these unwanted energies. One of the best ways to release it is by practicing the art of forgiveness—not just for others, but more importantly for yourself. Let go of whatever judgements and feelings of guilt, hate, envy, or anger you have toward yourself or others. Find whatever it is holding you back from happiness and release it. If you do not release these toxic energies, they will most certainly hinder your progress. Forgivingness is a constant process you must continuously practice. It opens your mind and heart to living the life you desire.

Notice when you have a negative thought or are thinking negatively. Write this thought down on the left side of your page. Write the thought or action which is opposite of this thought on the right side of the page. Think about it, meditate on it, and create an affirmation with this positive thought.

Take note of how your power to prosper multiplies tremendously after you have detoxed your mind. You will form the circuit of connectivity between your consciousness and the Universal "life force energy." Then, your new magnetic power of your consciousness will influence the static energy "ether" to convert it into dynamic energy "material form" for you to prosper.

Prepare to Prosper: Essential Skills
There are three tools to use as we go through the process of transformation:

1. Writing
2. Imagining
3. Verbalizing

We are the masters of influencing "ether" or "static energy," but in order to do so, we must clear all blockages preventing us from interacting with it. The three skills mentioned above are the tools you use to dissolve barriers and obstacles between where you are and where you want to be. You can mold and deliberately form dynamic and physical energy when you use these tools to remove blockages. That's when you begin to truly transform your life.

Prepare to Prosper: Showing Up

This is the mental gym where you train your mind to think of the things you want—not the things your mind wants to think about. This is the creating session where you get things done.

Before we begin, I cannot stress enough the importance of "showing up" to do the mental work. Regardless of how busy you feel you are, you must set aside the time to do the work!

If you have a problem showing up to do the work, you might want to write yourself an affirmation about it. For example, you can write *"I show up daily to do the work"* or *"I enjoy my creating sessions"* or *"I am disciplined with my creating sessions"* or *"I feel good when I am creating."* Repeat your affirmation at least three minutes or more daily.

Prepare to Prosper: Designing What You Want

Imagine yourself as a *consciousness design engineer*. Each day, you need to find a private place where you can go to focus your mind and energy on the life you desire. Use your imagination to expand your consciousness and begin to exude vibrations of positive energy. Paint a detailed picture of what you are seeing or doing in your new life and *feel* the emotions as though you have already achieved your desires. Then, let go and let the universe do its magic.

Be open to what the universe brings you! By now you already know your "sixth sense" or your intuition is a line of communication from God. Act toward the things brought to

135

you and be open to the field of all possibilities. Expect it. Allow it and receive it.

Keep reminding yourself there is a reward waiting for you. Supply will always follow demand. If you ask for it, there will be people, forces, and events that will show up to light up your path. Train your mind according to what you want and not what your outer reality suggests or the things you don't want. Create habits that will serve you and you will see change and transformation in your life.

The Road to Lasting Transformation: A Four Stage System
The new state of being "mindset" you want to create may be unfamiliar, uncertain and uncomfortable. But it will evolve and become more comfortable over time as you reach a deeper understanding.

In Diagram 9, you will see four stages of the mindset transformation process. This process is what you have been waiting for; this is the grand finale. It is applying everything you learned about yourself and your Divine hidden powers. Here you will see exactly how you can transform your life, create your own reality and become prosperous NOW.

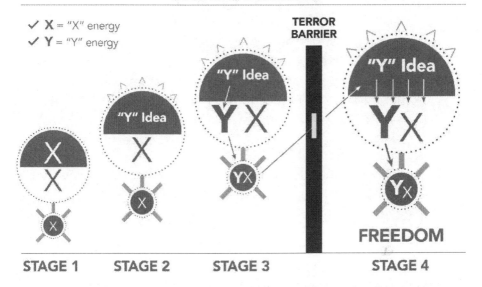

Diagram 9

In Diagram 9, "X" represents the current perception of your reality and **"Y"** represents whatever you want to be, do or have.

Imagine person **"X"** wants to transform to become person **"Y"**. For example:

- **"X"** is a person who makes $50,000 a year. **"Y"** is the same person who wants to make $ 50,000 a month.
- **"X"** is a person with low confidence. **"Y"** is the same person with high confidence.
- **"X"** is a person with health issues. **"Y"** is the same person with vital health.
- **"X"** is a person without a significant other. **"Y"** is a person in the right relationship.

"X" represents "X" energy and "Y" represents "Y" energy

Our main objective is to open the door to the subconscious mind. Here, we can plant the seed of what we want in life using the mind-power techniques (seeding, visualization and affirmations), then let go and let the universe do its magic.

There are four stages to create anything you want
Stage one: Look at Diagram 9. There is an "X" person getting "X" results. This person is experiencing and attracting certain circumstances, events and people representing more of the "X" energy. It is the "X" paradigm.

This stage is where thinking becomes feelings, and feelings feed corresponding thoughts. Because of this cycle, the person stays in the same state of being. They appear in bondage. There is no change.

Stage two: "X" person decides they want to be a "Y" person. He or she will start to infuse themselves with "Y" energy and show up daily to do creative sessions of matching their energy of how they will feel once they achieve it, creating "Y" vibrations. However, guess what happens to the "X" person? *NOTHING, There's no change!*

At this stage, he becomes conscious of his unconscious thoughts and beliefs. He wants a change and transform to what he wants to be, do, or have. He changes his thoughts and shows up to do the daily sessions, but his reality is still the same. It has not changed.

Most people will quit here. They get frustrated and give up. Recall the law of gestation; there is an incubation period during stage 2, just like a vegetable garden or a baby in the womb. *Manifestation will not happen instantly!* There is a delay of reflection of reality, which is what's happening at this second stage.

Understanding the time delay is important, but it is just as important to realize if you stay on this course long enough, and do the daily sessions, you will get results you desire as long as you don't quit!

You see, most people are unaware when they set out to achieve a goal, that it begins in the conscious mind. Which is responsible for about 10% of achieving the goal. The other 90% of the responsibility lies in the subconscious mind where people hold firmly to their beliefs and habits. People cannot achieve their goals just by using their conscious mind. They must delve deeper into the subconscious to reprogram their paradigm and create new habits to obtain what they want.

This is the red eyedropper example. This is the creating session where you are seeding, injecting, and infusing yourself with the images and feelings of the things you want. It takes time, and time varies from one person to the other based on how resistant the analytical and critical the subconscious mind is to accept the things you want as *truth*. Don't give up! Keep doing the daily sessions as instructed no matter how long it takes. It will get easier.

Stage three: This is a very crucial stage. During this stage, the person will have mixed vibrations of "XY" feelings in the form of confusion and mixed results. Sometimes they notice it is working, and other times it's not. Sometimes they feel good, sometimes not. It is mixed and very tricky to understand. One minute the person feel's confident and the next they are overwhelmed with doubt and worry. The difference between stage 2 and stage 3, however is by this stage in the process the person is resilient and aware of the thickness (analytical & critical mind) of the door standing in the way between the conscious and subconscious mind. With practice the person is trained on how to execute the mind-power techniques as well as how to trust the process—no matter how long it takes!

Stage Four: The people who make it to the fourth stage have demonstrated exceptional dedication in consistently showing up to the mental gym. As they continue showing up to the creating sessions, the "consciousness" scale begins to tip.

The law of cause and effect plays a major role here to break through the terror barrier (the analytical mind) from stage 3 to stage 4. The analytical mind must become weaker and weaker to break through into freedom.

When you set a goal—the amount of money you want, for example $50K per month—this is the *EFFECT*. It's not enough just to know it. You must picture if, feel if, and imagine what the $50K a month will do for you in terms of feelings and lifestyle. You need to focus your energy on the *activities* and *behavior* of what produces the *EFFECT*. The activities and behaviors are the *CAUSE*.

At stage 4, your "XY" energy is turning into "Y" energy. The laws of the universe are working for you. You become the "Y" person with a new state of being, mindset, and paradigm. You are experiencing harmony with the mind, body, and soul to manifest your future.

Keep in mind, however, you will never completely eliminate the "X" energy. All you have done is reduced its power source to the point where it becomes very weak. You have now plugged your power source into your "Y" energy.

Remember, as you go through these stages, you need to act in the world of possibilities—continually *expecting* and *allowing* things to happen in your life. This is when you will be doing things in a certain way of energy to open your mind and heart to prosperity. And, that, my friends, is The Prosperity System you now hold in your hand.

In my coaching sessions and workshops, people from all walks of life attended and absolutely love this transformation presentation. When we're in person and have more time, I can go into a lot of details to help deepen everyone's understanding of the transformation process. We have exercises to help everyone use the tools and do the practice—all while making it a fun experience.

The focus and collective energy of the people in the room, helps everyone move forward faster and further to gain a deeper understanding of The Prosperity System. It's fun to watch the "aha" moments when people work the system.

I hope you can join us in one of our workshops soon to expand your knowledge. You'll experience the collective energy of the group and gain a deeper understanding of the system to help you get what you want in life.

CHAPTER FOURTEEN
Taking Action

You've reached the point in this book where it's time to take actionable steps toward true transformation. Be patient with yourself and stay committed to the process.

System Implementation

You must follow this system in order to accomplish anything you want. In chapters 1-13 you elevated your awareness to your Divine hidden power and learned how to use this power. You were then given several simple tools and techniques to train your mind to believe what it takes to transform your life.

Now, it's time to get started by following these four steps:

1. **Discover Your Purpose:** What do you really want to happen in your life? Write down your purpose, vision and goals. If necessary, refer to Chapter 10.

2. **Plant the Seeds:** Emotionalize your purpose. Add the colors, sounds, and feelings that support your purpose—as if it has already happened. Use the tools found in Chapter 11 of seeding, visualizing and affirming.

3. **Live in Conscious Awareness:** Constantly be aware of where you are on the scale of consciousness between ignorance and knowledge. Imprint and understand how each side of the scale impacts you on a

physiological and vibrational level. See Chapter 12 for more clarification.

4. **Exercise Your Power of Choice:** Recognize that each moment is both an opportunity for creation to make progress or to experience a set-back. In Chapter 7, we discussed the laws of the mind, including reasoning and will. Remember your reasoning faculty is what gives you the ability to choose, and your will is what keeps you on track.

Change doesn't always come easy—nor does it happen overnight, even though it can happen quickly. It's your job to refer to the laws and principles of the mind and implement them into your daily creation session.

You will not transform your life overnight, although it is possible to see immediate changes at times. With persistence, practice and dedication to using the tools and techniques in the prosperity system, you will transform your life and embody your ideal self. When you begin to experience the transformation, you will be unstoppable!

Action and persistence are the keys to achieve what you want in life. That's the difference between the day dreamer and the achiever. Being in tune and having the awareness of what's happening around you comes first. Then, you will be able to organize the pieces of the puzzle by doing the right things, at the right time and in the right order to create the life you desire.

> **Bonus! You will find a Four Week Prosperity Boot Camp in the Appendix.** Use these detailed weekly exercises to jumpstart your journey to prosperity.

CHAPTER FIFTEEN
Infinite Potential

You have reached the end of the fundamentals of the system. You are ready to begin a beautiful journey to take charge of your life. I have provided you a complete system to accomplish anything you want. In this system, I provided you with mind-power techniques, principles, tools, and laws of the mind. And, I taught you how to develop certain qualities such as confidence, courage, persistence, determination, and decision-making to name a few.

We are all unique in this beautiful world. You are unique in your thoughts, ideas, understanding, opportunities, and in everything you do. There is no one exactly like you. You have Divine powers within you and unlimited power to be, do and have anything you want in life.

You have everything you need to create, and it's time to start thinking and dreaming *BIG*.

Big thinkers always know where they are going, but not necessarily how to get there. But they do know one thing for sure: *They WILL get there.* They have faith and confidence in their belief system and are flexible on their journey in getting to their goal. Remember, being flexible is also very important.

Big thinkers are exciting, adventurous and passionate people. They are in control of their thought process and have a strong mental image of what they want in life. They also know that with achievement comes struggle, pain and disappointment— but they don't let it defeat them! They understand it is part of the process and they have confidence that they will overcome anything thrown their way.

Big thinkers are also not afraid to ask for help. They are constantly doing, learning and developing themselves. They are consistently practicing the mind-power system. They have their own mastermind group to call on for help as well as their coaches and mentors to help infuse themselves with wisdom, information and insights. These are key ingredients to their success.

I don't believe you picked up and read this book by accident. I believe we were destined to spend time together through this writing, and hopefully in person sometime in one of our seminars. I believe you were ready to receive this valuable information. It is the Law of Attraction at work.

I want to provide you with some additional easy steps to take to ensure you take the actions necessary to achieve the life you want.

Start Each Day on the Right Path

Every day is either a successful day or a day filled with disappointment. It boils down to our vibration of energy to start with, and the affirmations we insert into our mind in the early hours to set the mood and the tone for the day.

You must remember each day consists of doing things, and you should do them in a certain way with specific energy and strong feelings to make your actions effective so the results will be strong and effective as well.

When you first wake up in the morning, what are the first thoughts that first come to your mind? What words do you speak first? Do you complain or worry about the day ahead of you? Do you think of the challenges and the problem waiting for you? Or are you excited for the possibilities available to you? Are you grateful for a wonderful night's sleep and the positive things in your life?

What do you say when you first look in the mirror, or when you're are getting dressed? What do you say to yourself when you're driving to work? Your day is controlled by the first thirty minutes of your day. It sets the tone and the mood for the day. To set a positive tone each day, repeat the following affirmations when you first wake up:
- ✓ "I am thankful and grateful for good and relaxed sleep."
- ✓ "It is going to be a great day.

When you look in the mirror, say to yourself: "*I love you* and *I feel great* and *I look great*" and "*I am going to create and design a great day with my thoughts.*"

This will transform your life and most importantly cause you to be in an attitude of gratitude —to be thankful and grateful for all the good things in your life. In doing do, we will get more of what we are thankful and grateful for. It is simply the law.

I love what John Wooden said: *"Make each day your masterpiece."* The way we make it a masterpiece is by doing our daily mental gym of creating new brain cells of recognition of how we want things to be. The key to success is doing the creating sessions on daily basis. It's important to show up and do them regardless of anything going on in your life. It's the eyedropper effect.

Of course, take time to read or listen to other self-improvement education to stay inspired with fresh thinking. Return to the Appendix or other chapters of this book repeatedly to reinforce your level of understanding, allowing this practice to continually transform your life.

Reduce your intake of news and replace it with listening to motivational speakers. There are many wonderful speakers available for free in YouTube. You can find the motivational speakers who resonate with you and listen to them as you're getting ready for your day!

Suggestions to End Each Day

✓ Review the current day's to-do list. See what you accomplished. Write a new to-do list for the next day. Make sure to include specific action steps to support your goals.

✓ Think about the day's events and what you have learned from them. Determine how you can apply this gained knowledge to the following day.

✓ Keep a journal documenting your progress toward your goals and the completed action steps. List success stories and other events from which you can learn and grow.

✓ Review your goals and analyze the progress you have made toward them. Tweak and adjust actions steps and remember, flexibility is power.

✓ Read or listen to self-improvement training to keep yourself fresh and inspired.

✓ Use the mind-power techniques of seeding, visualizing, and affirmations just before going to sleep and be grateful and thankful for a great, relaxed night of sleep in advance. Anything you think about just before going to sleep will be the focus the subconscious mind will have for the duration of the night. Ask specific and good questions of your subconscious mind to work on to get good answers.

✓ Keep a journal next to your bed to write down ideas that might come to you in the night. Many of our best ideas
148

come to us during the night. Make sure to write them down so you don't forget them.

✓ Do your daily mental gym to create new cells of recognition of how you want things to be. Remember to feel how it will be to be the person you've designed for yourself.

It is important to ask questions, just before you go to sleep. Sleep is a Divine gift. There is a reason why we go to sleep other than just relax our body. Sleeping helps to regenerate our organs, particularly our detoxing organs and brain. Sleeping gives our mind time to unite the subconscious with its higher self during restful sleep. Basically, we can reconnect with our oneness. In this process, we become one with the source of Divine power. We access the wisdom and the knowledge of the universe.

While we are sleeping, many answers come to us; whether in the form of dreams or in different ways of communications.

Our body heals better while we are sleeping. There is magic that happens when we are asleep. Anything we think about in detail and intensity before we go to sleep will be the dominating force during our sleep.

Answers may or may not come during the night you asked the question. They can show up any time. If it does not show up fast enough, repeat the questions again and be patient.

Simple steps to determine your beliefs:
1. Write down the most important things to you in your life. These are your values, principles and things that mean the most to you. For example: If it is important for you to be a good parent, then this is one of your values.

2. List the expectations or things you feel you must accomplish or do to live up to or support those values.

The measurement you set for yourself is your belief. So, for us to be a good parent, for example, we must spend a certain number of hours a week with our children. That's our belief which determines whether we meet our value of being a good parent or not.

Sometimes you will find the beliefs you have don't allow you to fully live up to your values. In other words, your values and beliefs could conflict with one another.

Any belief in conflict with your values must be eliminated or changed. For example: Ask yourself this question... "What is the reason I have not accomplished   my goal?" Then let the answers flow into your mind.   You will then discover the reasons why.   Remember, any statement that comes after *"BECAUSE"* is a limiting belief.

Recommendations to change or deactivate limiting beliefs:
First, you must build new brain cells of recognition that will better serve you. You can do this by following these steps:

1. Define the belief you would like to change.

2. Become aware this is a limiting belief and must be changed in order to move forward.

3. Replace the limiting belief with a new empowering belief. Write it down. Contemplate it. Then write down the benefits and the feelings you enjoy from adopting this new belief.

4. Associate great pleasure with the acceptance of the new belief and the benefits you will experience to transform your life. At this point, you are creating the matching energy for the things you want by using the law of vibration.

5. Use seeding, visualization and affirmations for the new belief. Repeat it over and over until you have created new cells of recognition, which is structured energy. Then imagine how you will be changed in a positive way once the new belief is in place. As you visualize and seed the new belief repeatedly, your subconscious mind will pick up the vibration of the new belief and will start to move events, circumstances, forces and people to help you get what you want.

You must have goals in order to achieve them!
If you do not know where you are going, how can you expect to get there?

Without goals, how can you determine whether you have reached your destination?

Establishing goals has a positive impact on our life. Goal setting provides a way to keep your life direction in check and a way to measure your progress.

Goals are pieces of your vision that must be accomplished for it to become a reality. Most people never accomplish their goals because they have adopted a holding pattern of vibration which does not match with the things and desires they want to happen. It is not aligned correctly with their beliefs.

As a result, the energies oppose each other and create dissonance rather than harmony.

We must have personal, health, spiritual, material, career, self-development, and financial goals.

Here are the important steps to the goal-setting process:
1. **Take each goal category and list specific goals for that area.** For example, examine your financial situation. Write everything about your financial development that you can think of as a goal without

thinking about how you will accomplish them or without considering any other limitations that would keep you from accomplishing your goals. *Ask yourself, "what do I really want?" Not, "what can I get?"*

2. **Define each goal.** By defining them in terms that are both specific and measurable, you will direct what you should be focusing on to reach your vision of the person you want to become.

3. **Assign a time frame.** Give each one of your specific goals a deadline to accomplish. Goals can be accomplished on or around this date and can also be extended if necessary. This is very important to understand because the universe cannot be forced into a time frame. But you must start with an expectation of time to move things forward.

4. **Choose your favorite goals.** Look at all the goals you want to accomplish within a one-year period. Choose the one in each category that you feel the strongest and most passionate about; the one that will compel you to act.

5. **List the reasons why you are committed to achieving each goal.** These reasons should be strong and powerful enough to drive you into action. But you do not need a full plan of action now.

6. **Break each goal down to a set of manageable objectives**. You have already planted the ideas or thoughts into your mind. Therefore, your mind will begin attracting the forces, people, and circumstances to help you achieve your goal. Listen to your inner voice and be aware of its development.

- ✓ Make sure you are monitoring and journaling what comes to mind for evaluation using the reasoning tool of accepting and rejecting ideas or plans.
- ✓ Brainstorm by focusing on your goal and by using the law of learning and asking yourself quality questions regarding the how, why, when, what and who of accomplishing your goals to further develop the plan.
- ✓ Ask yourself what is preventing you from achieving your goals. Write down everything that comes to mind.
- ✓ Analyze your discoveries of what is preventing you from achieving your goals. Write down the possible solutions that exist for overcoming these obstacles. This will become your new belief system that needs to be installed.

7. **It is time to take constant action.** If some of your plans seem ineffective, then try others. Notice what is working and what is not. Then press on with action until you accomplish your goal.

8. **Be persistent, do not give up.**

9. **Review your goals daily.** This repetition influences your subconscious mind to express the dominating thoughts of your goals through constant review. Your subconscious mind will pick up the desired thoughts and will start moving you toward your desired goals.

Seeding and visualization is the key to achieving your goals. Make sure you see, feel and act in a certain way of energy throughout the process to attract all that is needed for you to get what you want.

Now the question is this: **You now have this information and knowledge in your possession, what are you going to do with it?**

I hope you use it and share it!

We have come to the end of the journey with this book, but it is only the beginning of our relationship! I hope you go to my website, Powerbiz.com, and download the Question and Answer Segment I created for you to continue the work. You can also learn where I will be presenting the Prosperity System. I hope you can join us at one of our seminars near you or on one of our Prosperity System Cruises! Remember, to create the life you want, you have to invest the time and work to make it happen. Please do the work in the Appendix to create your prosperous life.

I invite you to take the ***next steps*** in your life and become the ***cause*** of your prosperous new life.

APPENDIX A
Prosperity Affirmations

Expanding your vocabulary is the first step

You will realize who you become in life is a function of the words you speak. The words you speak are there for you to invent and reinvent yourself again and again. You are constantly creating, whether you're doing it consciously or unconsciously. In other words, the universal mind takes directions from the words you give it.

So, it is important to have great vocabulary to be able to communicate effectively. As Rudy Kipling said, *"I am by nature a dealer in words, and words are the most powerful drug known to humanity."*

Words can be stronger than drugs to humans. They have an amazing effect on animating the force within us. They trigger pictures, images, feelings, and reactions to what they might mean regarding the structured energy and the cells of recognition that we have stored.

Words are our primary channel of communication. More importantly, words have meanings, pictures, ideas, feelings, action, and reactions attributed to them.

It is important to develop a strong and diversified vocabulary, as words affect and can determine our level of personal power. The words we use tell a story about our character and who we are. Words are the song of our life. Always use positive words and affirmations. Eliminate negative words that undermine progress toward your goals.

It's a great idea to implement a program that works to help strengthen and develop your vocabulary. A high-level outline of the program would include the following actions:

1.   Create a list of words to be used in different areas of your life.

2.   Develop a list of words for business purposes and for social and personal uses.

3.   Learn a few new words on a weekly basis and make it a point to use them in context throughout the day.

Your words are the key to opening and revealing your thoughts. The words and phrases you use will determine the effect you have on people and your environment. Your choice of words will affect your destiny and all aspects of your life.

Action Words for Affirmations

To love, to help, to transform, to learn, to study, to succeed, to answer, to share, to feel, to experience, to live, to choose, to grow, to serve, to commit, to act, to invent, to confront, to face, to be effective, to be flexible, to take on, to practice, to activate, to allow, to create, to operate, to restore, to transfer, to communicate, to dream, to organize, to effect, to understand, to escape, to teach, to take care, to reveal, to confess, to shock, to connect, to teach, to convey, to explain, to clarify, to simplify, to save money, to save lives, to shift, to build, to listen, to seek, to offer, to open, to communicate, to persuade, to respond, to establish, to align, to influence, to convince, to reflect, to match, to improve, to feel, to value, to make, to discuss, to talk, to negotiate, to free, to picture, to give, to simplify, to boost, to empower, to infuse, to fuel.

Add your favorite actions words here:

_____

_____

_____

_____

_____

SAMPLE AFFIRMATIONS USING POSITIVE WORDS:

I am successful.

I am confident.

I deserve success.

I deserve the best of everything.

I feel good about myself.

I love who I am.

Money is constantly flowing into my life.

I have an abundant life.

I am disciplined in everything I do.

I love life.

Life is good.

I am grateful and thankful for a great life.

I love and respect myself.

I attract the right people into my life.

I am a persistent person.

I am aware of my Divine power.

I have unlimited power.

I have unlimited energy.

I am an action person.

I love selling.

I love working with people.

I enjoy meeting people.

I enjoy earning money.

I am healthy in mind, body, and spirit.

I am generous.

I am friendly and kind.

I have everything I need in my business.

I am calm and relaxed.

I am a great presenter.

I am a great speaker.

I have a lot of charisma.
I have a lot of courage.
I am a great communicator.
I am focused.
I have a lot of energy.
I have inner peace.
I have a deep understanding of my mind power.
I am very organized.
I am lucky.
I am a creator.
I am blessed.
I control my life.
I am a great listener.
I am fun.
I can do anything.
I love to help others.
I control my emotion.
I care for others.
I believe in myself.
I love me.
I love who I am.
I enjoy improving myself.
I respect who I am.
I have faith in myself.
I enjoy my freedom.
I have greatness within me.
I have a vibrant healthy life.
I am happy.
I am focused.
I am wealthy.
God is the source of my prosperity.
I am guided by God.
I am open to receive God's abundant blessings.
I am open to prosper.
I am open to receive.
Money is flowing to me continuously.
I am a great leader.
I am looking great.

I am responsible.
I am a deal maker.
I am honest with high integrity.
I have awareness of my oneness.
I have perfect memory.
I am constantly improving myself.
I love being in ......

List your own affirmations here:

_____

_____

_____

_____

_____

_____

_____

_____

_____

_____

_____

_____

APPENDIX B
Become a Persuader

Persuaders are Great Communicators

Persuaders master the art of listening. Listening is a valuable skill. When you are focused on the other person without preparing what you are about to say next, then you are listening and paying attention to what is being said. You will learn what is important to the other person through their words, which will create pictures and feelings as they express themselves. You will gain insight into their values and what type of energy they are radiating.

Persuaders know their first encounter is not about selling. Their first important thing to do with the other person is to build rapport and trust within the relationship. Many people go directly for the sale, which is not effective!

Keep in mind, people do business with people they like and trust. Persuaders understand values and how they can influence the other person's decision-making process, as they relate it to a solution that serves them.

Basically, they find out what they really want. What would they gain and attain from their product or services? How would they feel by having their product or services? Then, they provide it.

Persuaders are great at delivering their presentation with vantage points and opinions. They know they must be convinced, influenced and confident in themselves before they can influence and convince others.

Persuaders also know how to fire up their own imagination, enthusiasm, excitement, charisma, and personal power as they are presenting, and they are persistent with their mission and vision.

Persuaders are goal-oriented people. They see themselves successful in what they do. They do their affirmations and see and feel themselves as confident. They see themselves getting the job done.

The Power of Asking Questions

Asking questions is part of the process of contemplation to discover, clarify and find more information related to any subject. The quality of your life depends on the quality of the questions you ask.

Our mind responds best to pictures and questions of *what, when, who, why, where, and how*. These questions stimulate the thinking process and build on other thoughts and ideas, in order to create suggestions and solutions.

We are constantly asking questions consciously or unconsciously. And asking questions leads us to other important questions.

For example, when we go to a restaurant as we are looking at the menu, unconsciously we are asking ourselves, *what am I in the mood to eat today? What looks good? What should I get?* We are having an internal dialog with ourselves.

Asking questions is key to understanding who you are. There is no question without an answer. They both exist in the same locality, according to the Law of Polarity.

Asking questions is simply an evaluation process that opens the doors for us to learn more about ourselves and other subjects. If we don't ask questions, we never get any answers.

When we learn to stop and observe how we are feeling and ask ourselves, *what am I thinking now?* Then we will know what to do next.

Applying some of these mind-power techniques will transform your life when you ask *quality* questions.

Stimulate Your Thinking Process

Contemplation is the power of asking questions and stimulating the thinking process —again, by asking *what, when, who, where, why and how.*

What's more, when you write, you create more thoughts. Those thoughts create images. The more you write and think of the images, the more you get emotionally involved with the images. The stronger the feeling and the vibration, the more the body moves into action. And, of course, the reaction is the result.

Identify the situation or subject you want to think about. Analyze the situation by asking yourself the right questions related to the subject. Then be quiet and wait for the answers to come. Observe the answers without judgement. This process of asking questions is the most powerful method you can use to stimulate the thought process. That's how you build the big ideas that you need to create the life you desire. Asking questions helps you to become more creative.

Communicate Effectively with Others

You must understand who you are in order to communicate effectively and to understand others. I believe the more you can communicate effectively; the more abundance grows in your life.

When you speak to someone, clearly identify the outcome and the message you want to get across. Always make good eye contact when communicating in person. Understand and respect the other person's values and beliefs and then customize your words to fit the other person's perspective.

Be a good listener and show a genuine interest in the other person's subject of communication. Do not interrupt. Listen with respect and understanding. Promote two-way communication by allowing the other person an equal opportunity to share their views.

When it is your turn to speak, make sure to see the other person with the good they desire. You must see yourself serving and helping the other person. Be the energy of what you are trying to convey from this communication. **That's your secret weapon to be an effective communicator!**

Think, feel and act with a certain energy. It is the energy you are conveying to help the other person get what they want, and that happens only by asking questions and listening to what matters to them. They will feel your vibration of authenticity and sincerity. When you act from a place of genuine authenticity and compassion, you attract like energies unto yourself. As you help people get what they want, you will get what you want. It's the law.

Use the power of visualization to see yourself as an effective communicator. You will feel your power. Work from the end result in mind first. Work from the perspective that you want, to create a "win-win" outcome for all parties involved.

Be prepared before the meeting and use affirmations such as "*it is going to be great meeting,*" and it will be! Be grateful and thankful in advance of the meeting (not just after the fact). By doing all of this in advance as preparation, your subconscious mind will focus on this dominating image and feeling. This will help you become a better communicator.

The Value of "Life and Business" Coaching

Coaches help their clients weed out negative beliefs and instill the right beliefs to help their clients transform their lives and get what they want.

Coaches are artists. They are connectors. They create the future and pull the desired future out of the future into the NOW for their clients. They improve the client's relationship with reality. They see the potential for greatness and weakness in their clients, which can be their hidden, unseen strength.

Coaching used to be only for actors, singers, politicians and athletes, as these icons couldn't afford to be just average and ordinary people. They had to be great at what they do, and that's exactly what a coach can do for you. They can help you achieve abundance, greatness and prosperity.

High-level CEO's, presidents of countries, entrepreneurs, professional and ordinary people, young and old from all walks of life are getting coached or becoming coaches themselves because they see the value in it! It saves time, headaches, heartaches, pain, and money!

Coaches turn information into transformation by building strong and powerful practices of certain activities and NOT just theories. They go out into the world to serve and help others get what they want in any area of their life. As a result, coaches get what they want as well. That's how life works.

Ralph Waldo Emerson said, *"Our chief want in life is somebody who will make us do what we can."*

Corporations are waking up to the benefits of having coaching at all levels of the company. They realize the biggest assets they have is to develop people, in order to grow and prosper. They empower and encourage people to be creative, in addition to being responsible and accountable. It has been proven that coaches help to boost productivity and profitability. When people work in harmony, they create amazing and powerful ideas which translate into profits.

APPENDIX C
Four Week Prosperity Boot Camp

The following section has concentration and contemplation exercises to help you transform your life. Now that you understand the concepts in The Prosperity System, it's time to put that awareness and understanding to work in a systematic and effective way.

At this point of your training, your mind is not exactly happy or thrilled or excited about the new system you are using. You are forcing your mind to do some mental work it hasn't done before. It takes commitment, energy, time, and effort to change—but it's worth it.

You will discover that it is not easy to concentrate on one thing for a long period of time; especially with many repetitions. But it will become easier over time.

If you get distracted and drift away with your thoughts, just notice this is happening and bring your mind back by asking yourself questions.

Training your mind is like training your body. When training your body, you see your body is *out* of shape, and you want to get it *in* shape. Of course, you can eventually see the difference physically as you work toward your goal. But it takes time and commitment to physically change your body. Well, the same is true with training and changing your mind!

It's hard to see how your mind is out of shape mentally. How can you measure it? Your results in life are good measures. You may notice your results are not where you want them to be, despite working hard toward your goal. This is a good measure to see how much you are out of control, and how much work you need to do. When you first start concentrating and contemplating on your desired life, you are at your worst. But it gets better and easier every time and every day. Don't give up! Keep on taking these necessary steps to make the changes in your life.

Get in the habit of doing meditation daily. It will help you more easily slip into a state of relaxation and be in the *NOW* moment to infuse the structured energy into the things you want.

Below you will find a four-week *mindset reset bootcamp* guide. It's time to do the real work and stay committed to the practice!

WEEK 1

Write down the ten laws of the mind.

For 5 minutes every day:

Contemplate & concentrate on one or two laws every day. Discipline your thoughts and gain control of your focus. Then, write down your realization; the "aha" moments that came to you when you quieted your mind. Note your observations about each law and the potential gain you can have when you start applying what you know and experience their power.

1. Concentrate and contemplate the following affirmations:
   ✓ "I am in control of my personal power."
   ✓ "I am learning how to use my personal power to my advantage."
   ✓ "My personal vibrations (thoughts and beliefs) determine and create what happens to me."
   ✓ I am the cause of whatever I experience in my life.

2. Draw the XY person on a piece of paper. Focus on it. Imprint it in your consciousness and contemplate on it.

During each day of the week

Complete the following, as needed:
   1. Self-observations:

- ✓ Stop and observe your thoughts and your emotions. When you are happy. Sad. Excited. Fearful. Or whatever you feel.
- ✓ Do this several times a day as needed. Become familiar with how your mind works. Self-observe as many times as you need.
- ✓ Write down the good feelings, as well as the negative feelings in your journal. Make sure your focus is on the good feelings before you end the session.
- ✓ Use the mind-power techniques from this book to weed out and eliminate any negative thoughts.

2. Go over your notes daily.

Warning note: Don't let your mind talk you out of doing the exercises. The mind is naturally a trickster.

As I have said all along, I am going to show how to do the work, but you must *do* the work itself. We can work as a team. As you know by now, I have created the system to be easy and fun to use, with simple language. So, do the work it takes to achieve the results you desire.

MAKE IT A GREAT, PRODUCTIVE, HAPPY, AND FUN WEEK.

WEEK 2

Each day choose one quality in which you feel you are weak (such as confidence, your ability to remain calm, your discipline, persistence, your physical features, etc.).

For 5 minutes a day:
1. Concentrate and contemplate how you can improve this quality. Write down the quality you desire to have.
2. Visualize yourself having this new quality and the results you are reaping because of it.
3. Seed and make conscious affirmations around it. Feel the emotions of embodying this trait.

For example, if you chose confidence as the quality to improve, imagine what it feels like to have this quality in your life and visualize what your life looks like when you have embodied this trait. In your visualization, consciously affirm, *I am confident* and allow your body to feel the emotions associated with having confidence.

During the day
Complete the following as needed:
1. Self-observation:
   - ✓ "How am I feeling?" Answer the question in your journal.
   - ✓ "What am I thinking?" Answer the question in your journal.

2. Use the mind-power techniques to weed and eliminate the negatives.

3. Review your notes daily.

MAKE IT A GREAT, PRODUCTIVE, HAPPY, AND FUN WEEK.

WEEK 3

Part I (Continue the activity of Week 2)

Each day choose one quality in which you feel you are weak (such as confidence, your ability to remain calm, your discipline, persistence, your physical features, etc.).

For 5 minutes a day:

1. Concentrate and contemplate how you can improve this quality.
2. Visualize yourself having this quality and the results you are reaping because of it.
3. Seed and make conscious affirmations around it. Feel the emotions of embodying this trait.

Part II

Choose something in your life that you want to change (e.g. health, finance, job, location, etc.)

For 5 minutes a day:

1. Concentrate and contemplate how you can change this area of your life.
2. Visualize your life with this change and the results you are reaping because of it.
3. Seed and make conscious affirmations around it. Feel the emotions of how you feel because of the change.

Make a list of 10-15 memories that were powerful and positive and gave you a feeling of being successful, happy, strong, etc. This is your *Acknowledgement List*.

For 5 minutes a day:
1. Choose one of these moments and concentrate and contemplate how you felt during that moment.
2. Allow your mind and body to re-experience these sensations and thoughts as if they were happening now.

One of the reasons to do this exercise is to get into a "good feeling" zone. You are putting yourself in the NOW moment as preparation for the next step of visualizing the whole picture. You've learned about the NOW moment's power of creation.

For 10 minutes a day:
1. Visualize the big picture of who you are becoming across all aspects of your life
2. If, at any time, you experience negative thoughts, use the mind-power techniques to weed out and eliminate them from your visualization.

MAKE IT A GREAT, PRODUCTIVE, HAPPY, AND FUN WEEK.

WEEK 4 AND FORWARD

You have done the previous exercises. You know your weak spots and you have journaled your progress. You know what needs to be done and how to do it. You know the missing pieces, so you can fix them. Use the mind-power techniques to continue to make progress. Visualize, seed, and affirm to do whatever it takes to transform your weak spots. Make them strong so they can become effective assets for you.

Keep on getting better through focus and self-improvement. You are your best self-improvement project. So, enjoy the ride. Keep on learning and expanding your consciousness and awareness of your Divine power.

Achieve your vision and goals by following the prosperity system outlined here in this book.

You know about the laws of the mind and the tools of what it takes to transform your life. My favorite law is the Law of Cause and Effect. You can accomplish a lot when you understand and contemplate on this law! Use it to your benefit.

You see, you created the vision of who you want to become. You set your goals. But remember, the goal is the effect. You will accomplish your goals by focusing on the cause, or the activities and the behaviors that lead to the effect or "the goal".

From this point on, you will continue to do some of the exercises from the previous weeks, as well. Pick and choose whatever you feel like you need to improve. Concentrate and contemplate on them. Whether it's the laws of the mind or the tools of the mind—or whatever quality is needed. You will transform your life!

MAKE IT A GREAT LIFE!

ABOUT THE AUTHOR

Nabil Esfahani is an author, speaker, educator and entrepreneur at heart. He has built and sold many businesses, with a focus on commercial real estate, land investments, and other ventures including consulting in the cruise & direct selling industries.

Nabil believes what we think and believe will manifest in our life. He is passionate about the human potential for greatness and the unlimited abilities we all possess. He is the author of "ACTIVATE YOUR HIDDEN DIVINE POWER" which provides easy and simple steps for people to incorporate The Prosperity System to help them change every aspects of their lives.

Nabil's passion, enthusiasm, charisma and understanding of the mind and how the mind works, gave him the necessary insights to create The Prosperity System with clarity and understanding using the latest discoveries from quantum physics, neuroscience and his own personal experiences in life. He shows others how to reprogram their brain to lead to a more fulfilled and prosperous life.

Nabil conducts seminars around the globe on land and at sea. If you would like to learn more about these seminars, please go to his website, PowerBiz.com. You can also join Nabil's email list and download additional activities to support your journey and implementation of The Prosperity System by going to his PowerBiz.com website.